AIRWING ENTERPRISE

AIRWING ENTERPRISE

MICHAEL O'LEARY AND ERIC SCHULZINGER

OSPREY

AEROSPACE

Acknowledgements

In order to complete this volume, the authors had to call upon many individuals and we would like to thank the following: Captain Harry Rittenour, commander of the *Enterprise* at the time of our visit; PAO Lt Gordon Hume, the *Enterprise*'s capable public affairs officer; VS-21's commanding officer Glenn Main and executive officer Steve Hinson; VS-21's PAOs, Lt Rick Sprinkle and Lt Mike Berger; the Lockheed Aeronautical Systems Company and Scott Hallman and Rich Stadler; and all the officers and men of the USS *Enterprise*. We would also like to thank Jeri, David, Matthew and Lynn for their continued support.

Published in 1991 by Osprey Publishing Limited
59 Grosvenor Street, London W1X 9DA

© Michael O'Leary and Eric Schulzinger

ISBN 1 85532170 X

Editor Tony Holmes
Designed by Paul Kime
Printed in Hong Kong

HALF TITLE PAGE
Bright yellow start carts add a touch of colour to the drab grey aircraft on the deck of the USS Enterprise *(CVN-65). The deck of a carrier is a crowded place and movable equipment is designed to be as low as possible so it can be manoeuvred under or around aircraft with greater ease*

TITLE PAGE
Two VA-94 LTV A-7E Corsair II light attack aircraft prepare to launch from the Enterprise's *bow catapult two. These launchings are always extremely critical affairs, and the deckcrew check and cross-check each procedure leading to the launch. Nicknamed the 'Mighty Shrikes', the squadron's drab tactical camouflage is brightened slightly by the stylized shrike painted on the vertical fin*

OVERLEAF
As the catapult launch crew look on, one of their number oversees the linking of the shuttle and the nose gear strop. Once this vital procedure has been successfully completed, the green shirt will bid a hasty retreat

RIGHT
Resembling a pair of shark fins, the vertical tails of two of VS-21's S-3A Vikings catch the last rays of a setting sun as the Enterprise *manoeuvres far out in the Pacific. The stylized Viking head adds a touch of individualism to the unit's subhunters*

For a catalogue of all books published by Osprey Aerospace
please write to:

The Marketing Department,
Octopus Illustrated Books, 1st Floor, Michelin House,
81 Fulham Road, London SW3 6RB

Contents

A Proud Tradition

SINCE THE service's inception, the United States Navy has had a policy of continuing the tradition of a ship's name. Thus, as a ship was either sunk in combat or phased out of service, the name would quite often be transferred to a new vessel. The name *Enterprise* has been utilized by US Navy ships since the year 1775, and eight vessels have worn it. However, the last two ships that have carried the name *Enterprise* are the ones that burned their deeds in the annals of American combat history – and both have been aircraft carriers.

The first aircraft carrier to be named *Enterprise* was CV-6, one of three carriers that made up the *Yorktown* class. The keel of CV-6, the second ship in the *Yorktown* class, was laid down on 16 July 1934 at the Newport News Shipbuilding and Dry Dock Company. The country was still in the grips of the Great Depression and the ship building programme was a great boost to the hundreds of workers employed by the Public Works Administration. On 3 October 1936, the *Enterprise* was launched with the words 'May she also say with just pride: I have done the State some service', borrowed from *Othello* by Shakespeare.

After a thorough fitting out, the ship was commissioned on 12 May 1938 and sailed soon after to South America on an initial shake-down cruise. By this time, it was obvious to some of the clearer thinking naval officers that the building tensions in Europe and the Far East would lead to war – a war in which the United States would eventually have to enter. Accordingly, the men of the *Enterprise* undertook the working up period of their carrier with a great deal of zeal.

The time between the commissioning of the carrier and America's entry into World War 2 was also a time of tremendous transition for US carrier aircraft. When the *Enterprise* first went to sea, USN combat aircraft were primarily biplanes. During those few years of peace, carrier aviation progressed rapidly as squadrons received the first all-metal monoplanes, and the biplanes were relegated to second-line duties. New types like the Douglas TBD Devastator, Grumman F4F Wildcat and Douglas SBD Dauntless filled the *Enterprise*'s 809 foot wooden flight deck.

One of the primary aims of the Japanese sneak attack on Pearl Harbor on 7 December 1941 was the destruction of America's small, but vital, carrier fleet. Fortunately, the carriers were not docked at Pearl but were out on manoeuvres in the Pacific, thus escaping almost certain destruction or heavy damage on that fateful day. Tragically, Dauntlesses from the *Enterprise* flew into land at Pearl shortly after the attack and were mistaken for enemy aircraft, several being shot down and the crews killed by friendly fire.

The *Enterprise* and its sister carriers were quickly able to thwart the Japanese timetable for victory in the Pacific. Of the *Saratoga* class carriers, only the *Enterprise* would survive the war. The ship fought in all the major battles of the Pacific and became the most decorated of all naval vessels, becoming the only ship to be awarded both the Navy Unit Citation and the Presidential Citation in the process. During its four years of combat, CV-6 was awarded 20 Battle Stars. CV-6 was definitely battle weary when retired and placed in storage during 1947. Like so many other American weapons of World War 2, little thought was given to preserving the *Enterprise* and after years of storage, the 'Big E' was sold for scrap in 1956, thus negating the chance of preserving one of the most significant of all naval vessels.

The concept of the carrier air wing had proved itself during World War 2 and would do so again during the Korean War. The carrier air wing is a self-contained unit that features everything from attack to fighter aircraft. Given the mobility of the carrier, the air wing can be quickly deployed to virtually any hot-spot in the world, something that the Iraqi government apparently thought would not happen when that nation invaded Kuwait. The American carriers that deployed to the Gulf were able to effectively blockade all shipping in and out of that hostile nation.

After the Korean War, it was evident that bigger and better carriers were needed to respond to an increasing threat from the Soviet Union and to cater to the needs of a new generation of jet aircraft. The American defeats during the early portion of the Korean War were a stinging rebuke for a nation that ended World War 2 with 100 carriers in action. By the time of Korea, the Navy could only field seven large carriers.

Contracts for a new generation of ships were issued and the world would soon become familiar with the names of the different classes – *Forrestal*, *Kitty Hawk* and *Constellation*. Called 'super carriers' by the popular press, the ships were indeed potent weapons of war, carrying air wings that were mainly jet-powered and capable of delivering a wide variety of weapons, including nuclear bombs.

The concept of powering ships with nuclear reactors had taken hold during the 1950s (the above classes all operated on fossil fuel) and, as a concept, was workable. The Navy broke technological barriers with the submarine USS *Nautilus*, which, in 1955, began operations powered by a nuclear reactor. This form of propulsion was important for submarine operations since it meant the vessel could stay under the surface for extended periods of time.

Since the new generation of jets went through a lot more fuel than their piston-powered predecessors, the Navy began thinking about a nuclear-powered carrier. Since a relatively small amount of space was required for the reactor's fuel, much more jet fuel could be carried, giving such a ship relative freedom during intense operations. With nuclear power, a carrier would be able to operate at high speeds for extended periods of time. Also, the ship would not require the huge boilers for the conventional engines so the entire superstructure could be made much stronger. The immense power of the nuclear reactor also meant that steam could be supplied to the catapults without impinging on the carrier's overall performance. The elimination of the boilers also meant that there would be no funnel smoke to cause interference during operations or provide an additional reference point as to the carrier's location.

It was obvious that the cost of a nuclear-powered carrier would be more than that of a conventionally-powered ship. However, a great deal of this cost was accrued during the vast amount of research and development that went into proving this form of propulsion. The nuclear-powered carrier would be free from the problems of supply of oil and could steam for long periods of time at full speed without any need for refuelling.

Authorization to build the new ship, to be named *Enterprise*, came about in the Fiscal Year 1958 budget and the keel was laid on 4 February 1958 at the Newport News Shipbuilding and Dry Dock Company. The carrier was originally designated CVAN-65. The N was, of course, for nuclear and the A was for attack aircraft carrier, but this terminology was changed to CVN and the *Enterprise* was redesignated CVN-65 on 30 June 1975.

The *Enterprise* design was based upon techniques utilized on the *Kitty Hawk* and *Constellation* classes, but the superstructure of the ship had a very distinctive appearance since there were no funnels. Construction of the ship proceeded with few problems and the then CVAN-65 was launched with a great deal of ceremony on 24 September 1960. The *Enterprise* was the first carrier built in a dry dock rather than on a slip way so launching occurred by merely flooding the dry dock. Sea trials went smoothly considering the radical nature of the new warship and the *Enterprise* was officially commissioned on 25 November 1961. Bickering in the administration of John F Kennedy, and the influence of Secretary of Defense Robert McNamara, saw the five follow-on ships in the *Enterprise* class cancelled and the next two carriers, *America* (CV-66) and *John F Kennedy* (CV-67) (who had been assassinated by this time), commissioned as conventionally powered vessels. It would not be until the *Nimitz* class was authorized in the late 1960s that nuclear power would once again be incorporated into American aircraft carrier technology.

The *Enterprise* has had a long and colourful history and in this book we will take a look at the ship, its aircraft and its personnel. The *Enterprise* went into dry dock during late 1990 for a three-year refit and when CVN-65 emerges in 1993, the carrier will be completely modernized and ready for several more decades of distinguished service.

Air Wing Enterprise *at its best. The deck of an aircraft carrier is a place of extreme action as this photograph illustrates with a VF-213 'Fighting Blacklions' Grumman F-14A Tomcat accelerating down the catapult while a 'Green Lizards' VA-95 Grumman A-6E Intruder is prepared for launch from the forward catapult. Spotted in close proximity to the catapults and waiting their turn for launch are a VA-22 'Fighting Redcocks' A-7E Corsair II, a KA-6D tanker again from VA-95 and an EA-6B Prowler from VAQ-135 'Black Ravens'*

'Aardvarks' and 'Black Lions'

IT SEEMS hard to believe but the US Navy's main frontline fighter aircraft, and a warplane that performed admirably in the recent Gulf War, celebrated its 21st birthday in 1991! The prototype Grumman F-14A Tomcat, BuNo 157980, undertook its maiden flight from the company's Calverton, New York, runway on 21 December 1970 with test pilots Robert Smyth and William Miller doing the honours.

Even after the passing of over two decades, the Tomcat remains a potent weapons system feared by all possible foes. What is interesting, however, is that the Tomcat, unlike the USAF's McDonnell Douglas F-15 Eagle, has been operated on a very constrictive budget that has precluded many of the modernizations and updates which the Eagle has been fortunate to accrue.

The F-14 Tomcat is almost certainly the last of a long line of Grumman 'Cats – US Navy fighters that have made the world stand up and take notice. Fortunately for America, Grumman F4F Wildcats were in squadron strength when the Japanese unleashed their surprise attack on American forces at Pearl Harbor. Although outmoded in many respects, the Wildcats took on the best that the enemy could throw at them, and the plane and its pilots became heroes of many early air battles over the Pacific – including the Marines' famous last stand at Wake Island where Wildcats fought the enemy until every last F4F was destroyed, greatly upsetting the Japanese timetable for conquest in the Pacific. The Wildcat fought all through World War 2 and on virtually every combat front.

Other 'Cats followed including the powerful F6F Hellcat, the sleek twin-engined F7F Tigercat, the jet-powered Panther and Cougar, the radical XF10F Jaguar, the supersonic F11F Tiger, and then the F-14 Tomcat. The F-14 restored Grumman back to its position as premier supplier of quality fleet fighter aircraft, a tradition that had been broken by the Vought F-8 Crusader and the legendary McDonnell Douglas F-4 Phantom II.

The record-grossing movie *Top Gun* showed the F-14A as the master of air superiority, but the Tomcat's greatest contribution to fleet air defence is its outstanding ability to counter the threat of long-range supersonic cruise missiles, and their launching aircraft, in battles beyond the outer perimeters of fleet defence. This capability gives the carrier battle group the means to carry the war to a potential enemy's highly defended doorstep.

How and why was the Tomcat created? The F-14 had its basis of creation in the complete failure of the ill-conceived Grumman F-111B, the navalized variant of the General Dynamics F-111 series of USAF combat aircraft. Under the administration of President John F Kennedy, Secretary of Defense Robert McNamara came up with the concept of creating one type of aircraft that could carry out the job of fighter, bomber, and naval interceptor. General Dynamics and Grumman worked to the best of their abilities to create a basic 'core' aircraft which would have the growth and modification capabilities to accomplish all the required missions.

The F-111B was designed to be a 'missileer' – an aircraft that would carry an extremely advanced radar system and the new AIM-54 Phoenix long-range air-to-air missile so that enemy aircraft could be destroyed well before they became a threat to the fleet. After flying several prototypes, the F-111B was cancelled, the programme falling victim to the very risky venture of attempting to create an aircraft that would be ideal for both the US Navy and USAF (an almost impossible task). The F-111B's performance and handling characteristics left much to be desired.

Even before it happened, Grumman officials knew the F-111B programme would be cancelled as the design simply could not meet the specified requirements. The company began working on an in-house concept called Design 303 and, as events would later prove, this early work would be a boon for the Navy. The Vietnam War was escalating and the Navy's Crusaders and Phantom IIs were having trouble combating the enemy's 'low and slow' tactics, and this was something that supposedly should not have been happening.

The earlier variants of the Phantom II did not have an internal gun, relying on missiles for aerial victories. The missiles were not scoring the success rate the manufacturers had hoped for and dogfights were being won by opponents who were generally, and mistakenly, thought to be inferior. The fighters needed more fuel for longer patrols, more efficient missiles with greater range, and the fitment of an internal gun. Air combat over Vietnam would also prove the viability of cancelling the F-111B. The Navy needed a new fighter that would be bold in concept and victorious in action.

Naval Air Systems Command issued a request for proposals to the aerospace community for a new fighter and five companies responded. After considerable research, Grumman's Design 303 was picked as the winner of the VFX competition, beating some formidable rivals. The January 1969 victory was a challenge to Grumman to create a complex new warplane in the shortest time possible. Led by Michael Pelehach, the design team chose two Pratt & Whitney TF30 turbofan engines, AWG-9 track-while-scan radar and Phoenix missiles (these coming from the F-111B), variable geometry wings (popularly called 'swing wings' by the press and another feature of the F-111B), tandem seating for the two man crew, and combat-proven Sidewinder and Sparrow AAMs with an internal M61A1 20 mm rotary cannon.

In an amazing 20 months after being awarded the contract, Grumman rolled out the first F-14A from its Long Island factory. The first aircraft was lost on its second test flight following complete hydraulic failure and the gathered press was treated to a spectacular (and successful) low-altitude ejection by the two test pilots while the prototype was on finals. Flight testing resumed in May 1971 when the second development aircraft was completed.

As further aircraft became available, testing rapidly accelerated and the Tomcat (as the F-14A was named, following Grumman's feline tradition) was able to show some of its amazing capabilities. A Tomcat flying out of the Naval Missile Center (now Pacific Missile Test Center) at Point Mugu, California,

LEFT
With the nose gear fully compressed and the afterburners lighted (the TF30-P-414s pumping out 20,900 lbs st each), a Tomcat from VF-114 'Aardvarks' is just seconds away from launch. With wings spread fully forward, the Tomcat spans an impressive 64 ft 1½ in. Fully swept back, the wings span 38 ft 2½ in. This view shows the superstructure and the large AN/SPS-9 long-range search radar to advantage

ABOVE

While one crewman holds his helmet for a further bit of noise protection, a 'Blacklions' F-14A is given the launch signal. Other aircraft flown by VF-213 included the Douglas F4D Skyray, McDonnell F3H-2 Demon (this aircraft giving the squadron its first capability with the then-new Sparrow missile) and the McDonnell Douglas F-4 Phantom II. Formerly based at NAS Moffett Field, California, the squadron moved to NAS Miramar during June 1961, and took a quantum jump forward in fighter capabilities when they accepted their first Phantom II in February 1964

LEFT

The C-13 catapult rapidly accelerates an 'Aardvarks' Tomcat down catapult three. VF-114 was originally established as Bombing/Fighter Squadron 19 in January 1945, flying the Grumman F6F Hellcat and, later, the Chance Vought F4U-4 Corsair. Early in its history the squadron changed designations three times and, in 1950, became known as VF-114. At that time, the unit deployed aboard the USS Philippine Sea (CV-47) after the outbreak of the Korean War

fired a Phoenix and was able to hit and destroy a target drone 126 miles away. This would give a first-ever capability of protecting the fleet at extremely long distances.

The F-14A radar and weapon system could engage six hostile targets at the same time and this was proven when six targets were engaged in November 1973. The Tomcat launched six Phoenix missiles which were guided to the targets by the AWG-9 and four direct hits resulted. As weapon trials continued, one of the development Tomcats was 'shot down' and destroyed by its own missile! This curious incident occurred when a Sparrow failed to clear its mount and impacted with the fuselage.

The first unit to receive the Tomcat was VX-4 'Evaluators', the well-known operational test and evaluation squadron based at Point Mugu, California. The first VX-4 aircraft arrived in 1972 and extensive testing took place while VF-124 'Gunfighters', the Crusader Fleet readiness squadron (FRS), was picked for the training of future F-14A crews at NAS Miramar, this vital mission commencing in 1973.

With afterburners blazing, the Tomcat departs the Enterprise's flight deck. Tomcats are capable of being launched without the use of afterburners. While operating during the Korean War, VF-114 flew more than 1100 strikes against North Korean forces. After returning from Korea, VF-114 traded in its faithful F4U-4 Corsairs, powered by the reliable Pratt & Whitney R-2800 piston engine, for the new jet-powered Grumman F9F Panther and, later, the all-weather McDonnell F2H Banshee. 'The Executioners', as the squadron was then known, embraced the missile age with the McDonnell F3H Demon in the spring of 1957, this aircraft being able to tote up to four AIM-7 Sparrows

A Tomcat launch is a truly awesome spectacle when the aircraft is in full afterburner. Besides the United States Navy, the only air arm to operate the F-14 has been Iran. In order to counter MiG-25 overflights, and, as part of the Shah of Iran's dream to build a huge, ultra-modern military machine, 90 F-14As were purchased between December 1975 and July 1978. All except one were delivered (the final airframe on order being impounded in the US after the Shah's fall) and made operational by the time of the collapse of the monarchy in January 1979. Survivors of the 79 Tomcats became part of the new Islamic Republic Iranian Air Force, but it was hard for the new regime to maintain the aircraft and quite a few were shot down during the war with Iraq. It is not known how many, if any, IRIAF Tomcats are currently operational

A rather strange incident occurred during December 1972 when the entire future of the Tomcat suddenly became questionable as Grumman refused to take a Navy order for a further 48 aircraft. The company claimed they had lost $1 million apiece on the first 86 aircraft. This refusal caused much publicity in the press and the total package contract went back to yet another ill-conceived idea from past Secretary of Defense Robert McNamara. Grumman asked for a 20 per cent increase in contract price, claiming they would still be losing $23 million on the total programme. Grumman was able to submit new prices in April 1973 for 100 F-14s for the US Marine Corps. This contract would allow unit costs to vary from $10.2 million to $11.9 million in Fiscal 1974 dollars and would allow the company to show a Tomcat profit in 1975.

The first two fleet squadrons picked to operate the Tomcat were VF-1 'Wolf-pack' and VF-2 'Bounty Hunters', which were commissioned on 14 October 1972. The two squadrons went on to introduce the Tomcat to the operational fleet in September 1974 when the squadrons deployed aboard the *Enterprise*. This initial deployment was later rated as highly successful for such a sophisticated new aircraft, and operational figures showed the Tomcats exceeded availability when compared to the Phantom II squadrons based aboard the USS *Coral Sea* (CV-43) as both carriers covered the evacuation of Saigon (named *Operation Frequent Wind*) in April 1975. During this trying period, the North Vietnamese Air Force never attempted to engage the F-14As.

ABOVE

'Blacklions' and 'Aardvarks' F-14As fill the Enterprise's *deck. VF-213 joined Carrier Air Wing Eleven (CVW-11) in November 1965, and began the first of six combat deployments to South-east Asia with its Phantom IIs aboard the USS Kitty Hawk (CV-63). VF-213 began its transition onto the F-14A in June 1976 and, on their first Tomcat deployment, the 'Blacklions' set a new WestPac record of 526 Tomcat flight hours in one month. Establishing themselves as the 'Best in the West' by winning the first annual Fighter Derby, the 'Blacklions' also broke all existing gunnery records with 413 hits on a single banner in November 1981 – a record that stands to this day*

LEFT

With wings swept back at a maximum of 68 degrees (the wings can be set manually back 75 degrees for stowage), three Tomcats overfly the Enterprise. *The aircraft are fitted with 267 gallon external fuel tanks mounted beneath each air intake. The F-14A has a maximum unrefuelled range of 2400 miles*

Well secured to the deck after operations, an 'Aardvark' takes a break. In 1961, VF-114 was the first Pacific Fleet squadron to fly the Phantom II. Inspired by the resemblance between the new fighter and the popular 'BC' comic strip character 'Zot', VF-114 adopted the 'Aardvarks' callsign in 1963. The squadron made five combat cruises to South-east Asia and was credited with five MiG kills during the Vietnam War

ABOVE
This high-angle view emphasizes the sharp sweep back of the Tomcat's wings. The 200 series modex on the nose of the F-14A was assigned to VF-213 during its Enterprise cruise while the 'Aardvarks' carried a 100 series modex. In April 1982, VF-213 assumed an additional mission – Tactical Reconnaissance, and began training with TARPS (Tactical Air Reconnaissance Pod System). With the retirement of the North American RA-5C Vigilante and LTV RF-8G Crusader, the fleet did not have a dedicated recce capability and TARPS was created to alleviate the situation. Around 50 F-14As have been wired to carry the system. With the TARPS unit in place, the F-14 can still carry its internal gun and a Sparrow or Sidewinder on each of the wing pylons. The pod is 207.5 inches long and weighs in at 1650 lbs

LEFT
The bubble canopy of the Tomcat affords extremely good visibility for the two-man crew. The F-14A is, however, an 'old' fighter that has seen considerable service and its age is beginning to show. Severe 1991 budget cuts went against the improved F-14A + and F-14D variants and the future of F-14 production was in doubt at press time. Grumman has proposed a highly modified strike fighter variant of the Tomcat to replace the stillborn A-12 stealth strike aircraft

Over the next ten years, Tomcats would equip a further 22 squadrons, includ-ing the Atlantic Fleet Readiness squadron VF-101 'Grim Reapers'. Two squad-rons, VF-191 'Satan's Kittens' and VF-194 'Red Lightnings', survived only from 1986 to 1988 before budget cuts eliminated the units even before their first WestPac deployment.

In July 1975, the Navy announced that the 100 Tomcats scheduled for delivery to the Marines would now be transferred to the Navy inventory. The Marines had been looking forward to their new aircraft (to fill the gap, the Navy handed over Phantom IIs that were ready for retirement), and this deci-sion caused some extremely bad feelings between the two services. As a sop, it was agreed tht the Marines would receive the first squadrons of the new McDonnell Douglas F/A-18 Hornet.

The Tomcat finally got into combat on 19 August 1981 when two VF-41 'Black Aces' Tomcats engaged two Libyan Air Force Sukhoi Su-22-M2 *Fitter Js* over the Gulf of Sidra after the lead *Fitter* had fired an AA-2 *Atoll* missile at the F-14As. Both Su-22s were destroyed in an incident that provoked interna-tional publicity. Other combat action followed on 10 October 1985 as Tomcats from VF-74 'Be-Devillers' and VF-103 'Sluggers' off the USS *Saratoga* (CV-60) were vectored by a Grumman E-2C Hawkeye from VAW-125 to intercept an Egypt Air Boeing 737 that was carrying the terrorists who had hijacked the Italian cruise liner *Achille Lauro*. The Boeing was forced down at NAS Sigonella, Sicily, and the terrorists were captured and turned over to the Italian government.

During this same deployment, Tomcats from the two squadrons were joined by F-14As from VF-33 'Tarsiers' and VF-102 'Diamondbacks' off the USS *America* (CV-66) to cover the massive carrier strikes against Libyan surface-to-air missile sites on 24–25 March 1986. When the *Saratoga* withdrew and headed

ABOVE
The 'Aardvarks', in defiance of toned-down camouflage, wore bright international orange flight suits – a practice only recently given up due to the non-availability of new suits. Late in 1975, the 'Fighting Aardvarks' transitioned to the Tomcat and the squadron made its maiden cruise with the type aboard the USS Kitty Hawk *(CV-63) during the carrier's WestPac in 1978*

BELOW

Wearing International Orange flight suits and colourful helmets in spite of the tactical paint scheme on their Tomcat, Lts Jim Eberhart and Bill Padgett prepare to depart the Enterprise *for a combat air patrol. Since its first Kitty Hawk cruise with the Tomcat, VF-114 has deployed aboard the USS America (CV-66) and, of course, the* Enterprise. *The USS Abraham Lincoln (CVN-73), the Navy's newest carrier, is now the sea-going home for the 'Aardvark's' 35 officers and 235 enlisted men*

home, it was up to *America*'s Tomcats to provide cover for the retaliatory bombing of Libya on 15 April 1986. This raid was a direct result of a Libyan terrorist bombing in Berlin, Germany.

Tomcats added to their score on 4 January 1989 when two Libyan MiG-23MS *Flogger Es* were destroyed by Sidewinder and Sparrow missiles fired from VF-32 'Swordsmen' F-14As flying off the USS *John F Kennedy* (CV-67). It should also be noted that Navy Tomcats accidentally shot down a USAF RF-4C Phantom II over the Mediterranean during 1987.

When the Navy's guided missile frigate USS *Samuel B Roberts* (FFG-58) struck an Iranian mine on 18 April 1988 while operating in the Persian Gulf, the Tomcats of VF-114 'Aardvarks' and VF-213 'Black Lions' flew off the *Enterprise* to provide cover while Navy ships and aircraft attacked and destroyed Iranian naval units. Tomcats from VF-41 'Black Aces' and VF-84 'Jolly Rogers' flew from the USS *Nimitz* (CVN-68) in April 1980 to cover the disastrous attempted rescue of the Americans being held hostage in Iran.

The F-14 saw its most intensive action during the Gulf War and the repatriation of Kuwait by Allied forces. Tomcats operating from the massed carrier forces flew countless missions in support of the incredibly intensive Allied air attacks against Iraqi positions.

Throughout the Tomcat's career, attempts have been made to increase the fighter's performance. Even before the type joined the fleet, the company modified the seventh prototype during 1973 as the F-14B. This aircraft was fitted with Pratt & Whitney YF401-P-400 engines that had higher thrust but the programme was cancelled. Seven years later, this aircraft was brought out of storage to be once again modified. This time, the Tomcat was fitted with

General Electric F101 DFE engines. Production models of this powerplant, the F110-GE-400, would later power the F-14A+ and F-14D variants. A proposed variant, the F-14C, was never built but features from this design were later incorporated into the F-14A+ and F-14D.

It was obvious that the design needed improvement, especially in the engine department. Around 120 F-14As have been lost in Navy service and many of these accidents were due to engine problems. The TF30-P-412A was a constant source of problems but these engines were progressively replaced with the TF30-P-414A, which offered the same power but much greater reliability. However, the engine change was not the complete answer.

In 1984, the Navy authorized Grumman to build the F-14A+ as an interim step towards a better variant. The F-14A+ is equipped with the F110-GE-400 which offers greater thrust and improved fuel economy. The A+ is also equipped with a computerized fuel control system and improved carrier landing characteristics. After 636 F-14As and the unique F-14B were constructed, production switched to the F-14A+ and 38 new examples were built while a further 32 were modified from existing airframes. The first modified A+, BuNo 158630, flew during December 1986, followed by the first new-built F-14A+, BuNo 162910, during November 1987.

Initial testing of the A+ was carried out by VX-4 and VF-101, new and modified F-14A+ Tomcats being delivered to VFs -24, -74, -103, -142, -143, and -211, who turned in their earlier aircraft. The first squadrons to deploy with the A+ were VF-142 'Ghostriders' and VF-143 'Pukin' Dogs', who sailed on 8 March 1990 from Norfolk, Virginia, aboard the USS *Dwight D Eisenhower* (CVN-69). These squadrons were able to participate in *Operation Desert Shield* before the conclusion of their deployment. On 7 August 1990, the F-14A+ Tomcats of VF-74 and VF-103 set out aboard the *Saratoga* and followed the

ABOVE
'Blacklions' F-14A is positioned on the catapult. The 'Blacklions' were the number one F-14 squadron in the third annual photo derby, winners of the first RECCE rally and are current Quick Print record holders. The second squadron in each carrier air wing is deployed with two Tomcats modified to carry TARPS

RIGHT
The well-worn nature of the tactical paint scheme (which is touched up with quick bursts of spray paint) is seen in this view of a 'Blacklions' fighter as it is guided to the catapult by an aircraft handling officer (identified by the yellow helmet and yellow jersey). In September 1982, the 'Blacklions' began their first deployment aboard the Enterprise. *During Indian Ocean operations, the 'Blacklions' flew the longest tasked F-14A mission from a carrier when they completed a 1775 mile TARPS mission*

Eisenhower on station.   Just two weeks after the F-14A+ deployed, the first production example of what many believe to be the definitive variant of the Tomcat rolled out of the Grumman factory. F-14D BuNo 163412 is the first of what some Navy officials hope is a long line of new Tomcats. Development of the F-14D began in 1987 when three F-14As were assigned to the factory for modifications. These aircraft would be utilized as avionics test beds for the new variant, but one aircraft, BuNo 161867, was equipped with F110-GE-400 engines to become a full-scale development D.

The avionics and weapon systems capabilities of the D-model Tomcat are greatly upgraded. The Hughes APG-71 radar offers enhanced overland modes, high-speed digital processing, and improved target detection. Other improvements include a dual 1533B data bus, digital cockpit displays, two AYK-14 computers, digital stores management and inertial navigation, ALR-67 warning receiver, infrared search and track sensor, ALQ-165 jammer, and the Joint Tactical Information Distribution System (JTIDS). New armament includes the AIM-120A advanced medium range air-to-air missile (AMRAAM) and AGM-88A high-speed anti-radiation missile. New improved ejection seats for the two crew members are also fitted.

Funding has been allocated for the construction of 37 new F-14Ds and the rebuilding of 18 F-14As into D configuration (up to 400 aircraft could be converted). After rollout of the first F-14D on 23 March 1990, testing has been undertaken by VX-4 and the Naval Air Test Center, while first deliveries began to VF-124 on 16 November 1990 at NAS Miramar. The first operational squadrons to receive the D-model were slated to be VF-51 'Screaming Eagles' and VF-111 'Sundowners'.

However, in March 1991 the future of the Tomcat was pretty much tossed

BELOW
Their tails stuck over the deck, two Sidewinder-armed 'Aardvarks' Tomcats share some of the crowded deck space on the Enterprise. *The F-14A has an empty weight of 40,100 lbs, a loaded weight of 59,715 lbs, and a maximum weight of 74,400 lbs*

RIGHT
With the proposed consolidation of the American military in the light of massive budget cuts, the future of carrier aviation remains in some doubt, but at least two carriers will be cut from active service. The Tomcat has proven to be the best overall carrier-based jet fighter and the Navy hopes to be able to find funding for continuing the production of an updated variant of the fighter

to the wind when the US Navy formally terminated the F-14D remanufacturing programme, increasing the odds that the famed aerospace company would be forced out of the aircraft building business. At the same time, the Navy also terminated production of 24 General Electric F110 engines and spares for the dozen F-14As that were to become D-models. Also cancelled were the orders for the Hughes Aircraft Co AN/APG-71 radar.

Grumman is proposing to the government to take over the recently cancelled General Dynamics A-12 stealth attack aircraft programme. The flying wing had been terminated by Defense Secretary Richard B Cheney due to cost over-runs. Cheney, on the debit side, had also been pushing for the cancellation of the entire F-14 programme so it is unclear how he will react to the proposal for a heavily modified F-14 to serve in the ground attack role. At press time, the Navy and Grumman are fighting the cancellation because the Navy believes that the F-14 is one of its most effective and cost capable aircraft, while certain political representatives in favour of the F-14 have stated that the government cannot readily cancel a contract that is on schedule and on budget. Whatever the outcome of the massive Tomcat debate, it is clear that Grumman and the Navy have done themselves proud by creating one of the greatest naval aircraft of all time.

Ordnancemen prepare to install Sparrow missiles on a Tomcat. The F-14A can carry a formidable array of weaponry including the internally mounted M61A1 20 mm cannon, four AIM-54 Phoenix missiles mounted on pallets, or four AIM-7 Sparrows fitted in the under fuselage recesses. Two AIM-9 Sidewinders can also be carried on each underwing pylon, which can also carry one AIM-54, or one AIM-7 and one AIM-9. From the outset of the design, the capability of carrying up to 14,500 lbs of air-to-ground weaponry was built into the Tomcat, although the jet is only now being utilized in this type of mission by selected squadrons

ABOVE

An 'Aardvarks' F-14A slowly taxies across the deck of the Enterprise. *This extreme rear view illustrates how the tail hook fits flush with the tail cone, directly below the main fuel dump. The 1980s proved to be a significant decade for the 'Aardvarks' since the squadron won the coveted Fightertown Mutha Trophy, the Admiral Joseph Clifton Award, the Battle E Award, the High Noon Gun Derby Award, and the CNO Safety S award*

OVERLEAF

Few sights are more compelling than a Tomcat night launch while the aircraft is in full afterburner. The roar of the afterburners combines with the many other noises produced during carrier operations to create a din that makes the wearing of ear protectors mandatory. The jet blast deflector is raised to the full position for the Tomcat catapult launch

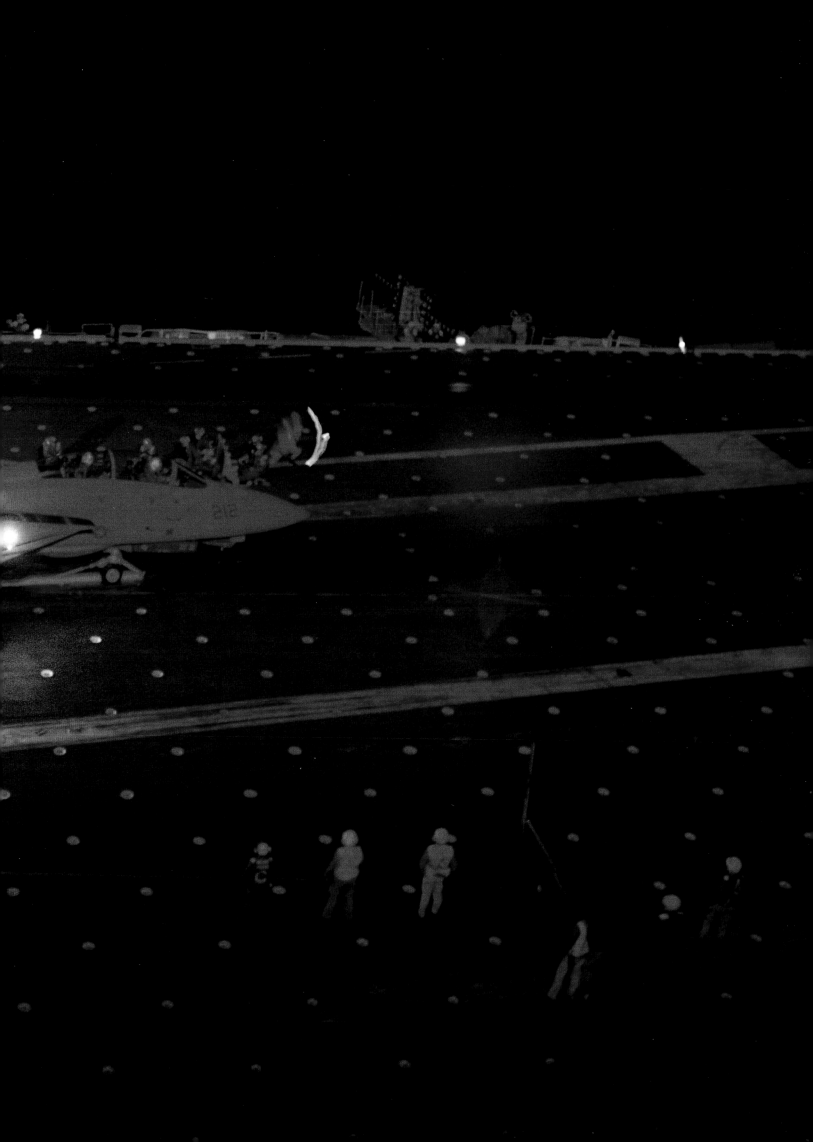

ABOVE

A start cart, one of several 'yellow gear' vehicles to be found on a carrier deck, positions a Tomcat that is carrying one Phoenix, one Sidewinder and a Sparrow missile. Maximum speed of the F-14A is 1544 mph at 40,000 ft; cruise speed for maximum fuel economy is 610 mph while initial rate of climb is 32,500 fpm

LEFT

Enterprise *airpower at its best. At the start of a day's flying activities, the carrier's deck is full of aircraft including Intruders, Tomcats, Prowlers, Greyhounds, Hawkeyes and Corsair IIs*

ABOVE

Before the Gulf War, Tomcats had seen considerable action in the Middle East area including many combat air patrols after the taking of American hostages in Iran. The first combat victories for the type occurred on 19 August 1981 when two VF-41 'Black Aces' crews shot down two Libyan Air Force Sukhoi Su-22M-2 Fitter Js after one of the Su-22 pilots fired an AA-2 Atoll missile at the lead Tomcat

RIGHT

While a fire crew looks on, a VF-114 Tomcat is towed into position. Threat of fire is always a major concern aboard any aircraft considering the vessel is usually fully loaded with jet fuel and a variety of high explosive weapons. On 14 January 1969, while operating off Hawaii, the Enterprise *was seriously damaged by a fire that destroyed a number of aircraft, detonated nine bombs, and did extensive damage to the ship's structure*

The mighty 'Hoover'

THE LOCKHEED S-3 Viking is one of the most important components of the carrier air wing since the versatile anti-submarine warfare (ASW) craft can take aloft the widest assortment of sensors and weapons for a carrier-based aircraft while enjoying the longest unrefuelled range (normal range is 2000 miles and the aircraft has an unrefuelled endurance of four-and-a-half hours while operating at a radius of 530 miles). This combination of factors gives the Viking the ability to protect the fleet from a variety of threats.

The Viking carries sensors that include Magnetic Anomaly Detection (MAD) for searching out submerged enemy submarines, Electronic Surveillance Measures (ESM), Forward Looking Infrared (FLIR), pulse-compressed digital radar, and 60 sonobuoys. The new S-3B conversion adds to this impressive package chaff, flares, imaging radar, a new acoustic data processor, and an ESM suite that is comparable to that on the EA-6B Prowler. The weapons bay and underwing pylons allow for the carriage of torpedoes, mines, cluster bombs, general purpose bombs, rockets, flares, and the deadly Harpoon anti-shipping missile.

The Viking carries a crew of four: Pilot, two Naval Flight Officers (COTAC and TACCO) and a Naval Aircrewman (SENSO), who is of enlisted rank. The SENSO is extensively trained in the analysis of acoustic signatures and his main mission is to configure the acoustic data processor for maximum performance and analyze the target's acoustic signature for both classification as well as determining track, speed and depth of the target. When the Viking crew is not engaged on ASW operations, the SENSO aids other crew members by taking over one or more sensors, or operating the Navy Tactical Data System (NTDS) Link-11.

The Tactical Co-ordinator (TACCO) matches the mission with the capabilities of the aircraft, tactical situation, and personal workload and experience. The TACCO occupies the right rear seat and deploys buoys and directs aircraft movement for further buoy or weapons release. By integrating visual and verbal information from the crew, the TACCO maintains the dynamic tactical plot. This visual information can be passed via Link 11, informing the battle group of new contacts or prosecution status, as well as receiving new orders.

The COTAC is an acronym for the function of co-pilot and TACCO. Both the COTAC and the TACCO undergo training as Naval Flight Officers in

Pensacola, Florida. Flying Beech T-34C Turbo Mentors, Rockwell T-2 Buckeyes, and Douglas TA-4 Skyhawks, the course lasts one year. During training, emphasis is placed on low-level and radar navigation, air sense, and air combat manoeuvring. In the Viking, a complete set of instruments and flight controls is available for the COTAC. The COTAC can back up the pilot, which is particularly useful on longer missions where fatigue can be a definite factor. Low altitudes, necessitated by the ASW mission, combined with co-ordinated operations between other ships and other air elements can lead to a quite precarious environment and the COTAC provides a needed additional set of 'Eyeballs, Mark One' to maintain contact with the air elements while helping the pilot with airspeed and altitude calls. The COTAC can also aid the TACCO with non-acoustic sensors and tactical communications while reducing pilot workload by operating the radios and weapons selection.

The new Navy pilot ('nugget' in fleet slang) can often face some daunting challenges when he is first assigned to a Viking Fleet Replenishment Squadron (FRS). Like all other naval jet pilots, the nugget has been trained in air combat manoeuvring, bombing, low-level navigation, and formation flight. However, the new ASW pilot must learn this specific mission, unlike the fighter or attack pilots. The new pilot must keep the overall 'big picture' of the mission. Trained in submarine tactics and capabilities, he must keep the aircraft properly positioned. Too close and he may alert the submarine, too far away and contact with the enemy can be lost before a new buoy is dropped.

Initial training for the Viking's crew members is separate, but they are all brought together at the FRS. VS-41 'Shamrocks', at NAS North Island, San Diego, California, was the sole FRS until the introduction of the S-3B. At NAS Cecil Field, Florida, VS-27 'Seawolves' is now training crews in the S-3B weapons system. Upgrading all east coast Viking squadrons to the S-3B will be complete by Fiscal Year 1991 if no new budget cuts are undertaken. West coast Viking squadrons will not complete transition until FY 92, except for VS-21 'Fighting Redtails' which began transitioning to the S-3B in October 1990 to become the first VS squadron to be forward deployed as part of Air Wing 14 aboard the USS *Independence* (CV-61) after the *Enterprise* went into port for overhaul.

During the ten-month Viking training programme, all S-3 systems are thoroughly covered and, during the last three months of the course, the new VS-41 four-man crew is put into the Weapon Systems Trainer (WST) where they put their individual knowledge and skills into practice. It is in the WST that the VS-21 crew develops the group co-ordination that is essential in operating a complex aircraft like the Viking in a combat situation.

Once the crew enters operational service with VS-21, the primary mission is, of course, ASW. However, the S-3A/B has developed into such a versatile aircraft that the crew is also capable of operating in such diverse roles as transporting captured terrorists(!), hauling essential carrier components several thousand miles from the *Enterprise*, and lugging sacks of mail from the shore bases to the battle group.

The Viking's ability to stay on station for lengthy periods of time allows the VS-21 crew to act as a secure communication relay between battle groups, or as the scene of action commander (SAC) in a search and rescue (SAR) flight.

VS-21's Vikings also have the provision to carry out inflight refuelling, either between themselves or with other aircraft of the fleet. This extremely important mission came about because of the S-3's low specific fuel consumption and the ability to bring untransferred fuel back aboard the *Enterprise* (some other refuellers have to dump fuel in order to lower landing weight before heading

PREVIOUS PAGES
With its two TF34-GE-400A turbofans running (9275 lbs thrust each), a VS-21 pilot carefully moves his Viking away from its parking spot under the watchful and helpful assistance of the deck crew. In such a confined space filled with so many running engines, care must be exercised at all times while operating on the deck. In 1964, the Navy, searching for a new anti-submarine aircraft to be based aboard aircraft carriers, circulated an Experimental Carrier-Based ASW aircraft (VSX) proposal among aircraft builders and followed, in 1966, with a Specific Operational Requirement for the aircraft. In 1968, a formal Request for Proposals was issued and the Navy asked a joint General Dynamics/ Grumman team and Lockheed to submit and further define their proposals

Shrouded by the mists of an early morning, VS-21 Vikings await a full day (and night) of flying under operational conditions. Although Lockheed had long been a leader in ASW aircraft, the company had little experience in building aircraft that operated from carriers. The company wisely combined resources with LTV Aerospace for their expertise in carrier-based aircraft, and with the Univac Federal Systems of Sperry Rand for their fund of knowledge in ASW equipment. The team considered a number of designs, but all were based on utilizing two General Electric TF34 high bypass ratio turbofans for power

back to the carrier). Also, the S-3 can hook up to other aircraft that are too heavy to land aboard the carrier and do a reverse fuel transfer, thus lowering the other aircraft's weight to acceptable landing limits and returning valuable fuel to the ship.

Most VS-21 missions can be generalized into three categories; surface search and control (SSC), strike warfare and ASW. In the SSC mission, the Viking's multitude of sensors, Link 11 capability and superb navigation accuracy make the aircraft ideal for the task. As for the strike mission, Commander Dave Architzel of VS-30 stated, 'In the past, in a strike on a hostile surface action group, we'd probably not play a role. Now, we're the detector, classifier and attacker. It gives the wing commander flexibility and increases the requirements for S-3 sorties.' It is also not uncommon to see S-3 squadrons flying strike lead in all-air wing mining exercises. S-3's integrate not only with the air wing, but also the battle group. For the primary mission of ASW, this interoperability is not only beneficial but necessary. The Viking is fully capable of working with the fleet's other airborne assets such as the P-3C Orion, SH-3, SH-60, and SH-2. This ability greatly increases track and attack capability.

Between operational deployments, VS-21 Viking crews maintain their cutting edge with training flights and plenty of work in simulators. Simulator instructors can programme just about any situation into the cockpit, causing the crew to work together under extreme stress. Engine failures, gear problems, threat situations – all these can be put into the simulator environment, causing the crew to either 'sink or swim'. VS-21 crews also hone their torpedo skills on specially instrumented ranges that record real time three-dimensional plots of the aircraft, submarine and torpedo. In the Viking, two tape recorders store the information from the practice mission. An analogue tape recorder (ATR) tracks signals from the buoys as well as intercockpit and radio communications,

ABOVE

For every flight hour spent by VS-21 crewmen, several more are spent planning and preparing. These Viking crewmembers are seen 'suiting up' prior to going 'upstairs' to their waiting S-3A. The first YS-3A (BuNo 157992) undertook its maiden flight from the USAF's Plant 42, Palmdale, California, on 21 January 1972. Piloted by Lockheed test pilots John Christiansen and Lyle Schaefer, the aircraft remained aloft for 45 minutes while standard systems checks were carried out

LEFT

Members of VS-21 brief an ASW practice mission in their ready room. Lockheed chose a traditional design for the S-3A (after considering such 'exotic' features as variable sweep wings) with a rather boxy looking machine that had a shoulder-mounted folding wing with a moderate 15 degree sweep and the two turbofans mounted in underwing pods set close to the fuselage. A prominent vertical tail was designed to also fold. Naval Air Systems Command reviewed the designs submitted by General Dynamics/Grumman and Lockheed and, on 4 August 1969, awarded the contract to Lockheed for six flight test and two static test YS-SAs

LEFT

Before any military flight, there are plenty of forms to fill out as can be seen. All eight YS-3As were put into an extensive flight and static test programme that lasted 26 months and included the many steps that a carrier-based aircraft must go through – including carrier qualifications aboard the USS Forrestal (CV-59) *in December 1973. However, the YS-3As were just three months into their testing trials when the Navy, in April 1972, placed an order for 13 S-3As. The service was confident that Lockheed had a winner and they wanted to get the new aircraft into service to counter an increasingly sophisticated Soviet submarine threat. Also, the S-3 would replace the Grumman S-2 Tracker that relied on highly-explosive avgas for its Wright radial engines*

while a digital tape cartridge records system parameters including navigation updates, buoy and weapon drop location as well as the configuration of the acoustic data processor and ESM equipment. After the actual flying is completed, the mission can be replayed to analyze the torpedo drop, and this aids in crew training and checking out the weapon system's performance.

When VS-21 prepares to deploy aboard the *Enterprise*, the squadron undertakes extensive training with the other squadrons aboard the carrier and with other ships forming the battle group. A typical mission could find the VS-21 Viking launched into the carrier overhead for mission tanking. As the pilot and COTAC handle the refuelling package, the TACCO and SENSO operate the ESM and Link 11, providing ESM information to VAW-117 'Nighthawks' E-2C Hawkeyes for passive intercept fixing. After the tanking portion of the mission is finished, the S-3 leaves the carrier overhead and flies toward an assigned surface search sector. If the sun has fully set, the COTAC utilizes his radar to vector the pilot to the next contact.

Once the S-3 is within range, the SENSO performs a radar to FLIR hand-off and classifies the contact, sending the information back to the Battle Group Commander over the secure high frequency (HF) link. In the submarine patrol area (SPA), the Viking is tasked to deploy and monitor a buoy field. Once the buoy field is deployed, the S-3 crew then goes back to the carrier overhead to take on fuel from the recovery tanker while the SENSO continues to monitor the buoy pattern and the TACCO reviews new ESM information. By performing these functions, VS-21 can provide the most up-to-date ASW and ESM cueing information to oncoming aircraft.

As the 'Fighting Redtails' transition into their new S-3Bs, they will create a new era of ASW and strike capability not presently available on the West coast. The squadron will be able to bring new meaning to the *forward* portion of forward deployed carrier battle group.

RIGHT

While the flight crews complete their final preparations, the maintenance crews make sure each aircraft is ready for its mission – even down to providing a bit of personal service like cleaning the S-3's massive windshield. The test regime of the Viking was remarkably trouble free and only one change was made to the basic design; the addition of small metal strips on the wing leading edge between the engine and the fuselage to help improve the aircraft's stall characteristics. An extremely successful contract, Lockheed went on to build a total of 187 Vikings, including the YS-3As. During August 1978, the last S-3A (BuNo 160607) was delivered but Lockheed has retained the tooling for the aircraft and the Viking could be put back into production if the need arose

LAU-126/A C-0002
N00163-84-C-0002
LOT NO 37

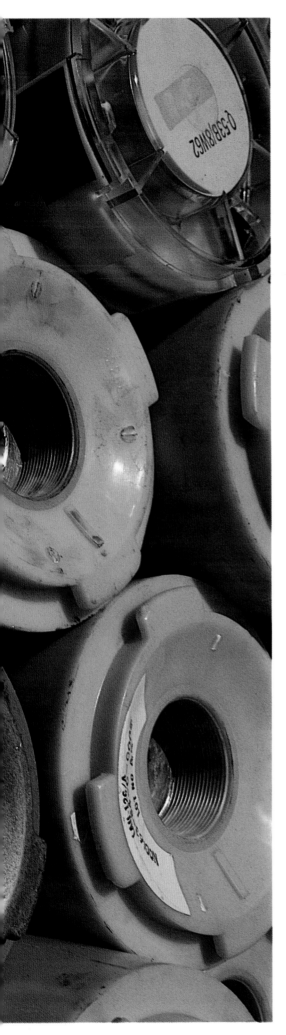

ABOVE
The first squadron to operationally use the S-3A was VS-21 who acquired their aircraft during July 1974 at Naval Air Station North Island, California. VS-21 scored another first when it took its aircraft aboard the USS John F Kennedy (CV-67) for the Viking's first operational deployment during July 1975. The 'Fighting Redtails' of VS-21 also became the first west coast squadron to operate the improved S-3B. This 'Fighting Redtails' crew is seen enjoying a few moments of light-hearted conversation before boarding their waiting aircraft

LEFT
The S-3A's primary acoustic sensors comprise 60 sonobuoys, which are used in conjunction with the Viking's other sensors that include a retractable tail boom with a Texas Instruments AN/ASQ-81 magnetic anomaly detection sensor (MAD), Texas Instruments AN/APS-116 nose radar, and, in a retractable belly radome, a Texas Instruments OR-89 forward-looking infra-red scanner (FLIR). Information is processed through the Univac AN/AYK-10 digital computer

PREVIOUS PAGES
Sonobuoys being loaded in the belly of an S-3A. As can be seen, the chutes for the sonobuoys are slanted towards the rear. The aircraft's bomb bay can carry up to 2000 lbs of offensive weapons including depth charges, bombs and torpedoes, while the wing racks can carry further weapons

There is no mistaking the location for this engine spool up, the VS-21 deck crew overseeing the pre-ignition procedures under the gaze of Enterprise's formidable island. A complex series of hand signals from various crewmen impart all the relevant information needed by the pilot to ensure that the twin TF34s fire up correctly

PREVIOUS PAGES

A setting Pacific sun highlights a trio of VS-21 Lockheed S-3A Vikings. This view shows to advantage the differences between the 'old' two tone gloss paint scheme and the newer flat grey with low visibility markings and insignia. The cleverly designed folding wing system on the S-3 allows for the aircraft to be stored in the minimum amount of space for an aircraft of its size.

Visibility from the Viking is nothing if not excellent, the huge windows and windscreen providing a virtually unobstructed view of possible surface targets. This angle also illustrates how closely the turbofans are mounted to the fuselage. The panels enclosing the other two crew members can clearly be seen behind the pilot's position. All crew stations are equipped with ejection seats

As a VS-21 S-3A is positioned on the catapult, the pilot begins to unfold the Viking's
high-aspect ratio wings. The Viking's internal fuel capacity of 1900 gallons is usually
supplemented with two underwing drop tanks, each holding 300 gallons. A retractable
refuelling probe can be utilized to extend the S-3's range even further

OVERLEAF
The Viking's wing spans an imposing 68 ft 8 in but can be folded to only 29 ft 6 in. The S-3's length is 53 ft 4 in while the height is 22 ft 9 in or 15 ft 3 in with the vertical tail folded. Total wing area is 589 sq ft. Maximum weight is 52,539 lbs, loaded weight is 43,491 lbs while empty weight is a mere (!) 26,650 lbs

BELOW
Close-up and personal, an S-3A prepares for a cat shot. One of the most critical phases of carrier operations, each cat shot is checked and rechecked before final launch. At 25,000 ft, the S-3A can achieve a maximum speed of 518 mph while the more economical cruising speed is 403 mph. Service ceiling is 35,000 feet and the rate of climb (initial) of the Viking is 4200 feet per minute. The maximum range of the aircraft with full fuel load is 3500 miles but the normal range is 2000 miles

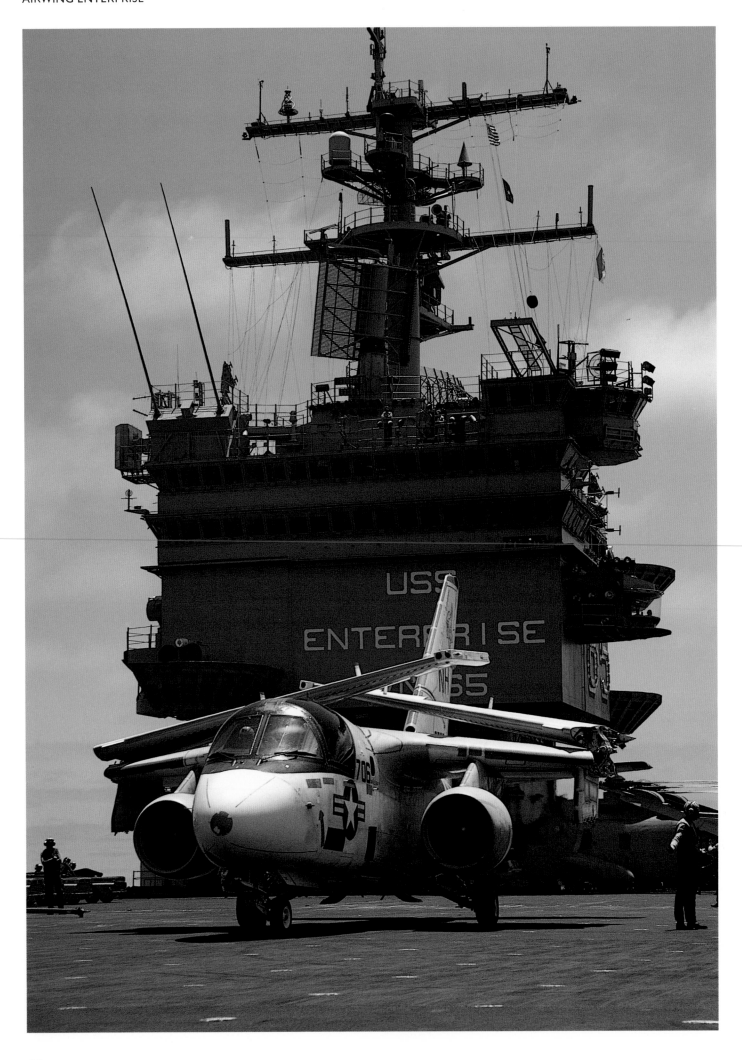

ABOVE
As an S-3A's wings begin to unfold prior to a cat launch, the very sturdy blast barrier is raised by hydraulic rams. Note how the small 'USS Enterprise' is carried above the Navy designation while an equally small CVW-11 is painted below VS-21. The blast barrier prevents damage to other aircraft by the launching jet's exhaust and also prevents any unwary deck crew from being blown overboard

LEFT
With the Enterprise's *bridge forming an imposing background, a VS-21 S-3A taxies to position. As S-3As are converted to S-3Bs, the older style paint scheme is replaced with the current in vogue low visibility scheme that is the bane of aircraft enthusiasts*

ABOVE

The launch is go! With a burst of steam from the catapult, the bridle begins to rapidly accelerate Commander Glen Main's Viking, momentarily pushing the crew back in their seats with a healthy application of G force

RIGHT

With the nose gear compressed fully down, a VS-21 Viking begins its short charge down the Enterprise's *catapult. The S-3 crew consists of a pilot, two Naval Flight Officers (COTAC and TACCO) and an enlisted Naval Aircrewman (SENSO). The SENSO, located in the left rear seat, is unique to carrier aviation – being the only enlisted person to fly in an aircraft with an ejection seat. The SENSO goes through extensive training in acoustic signature analysis. His primary mission is to configure the acoustic data processor for maximum performance and analyze the target's acoustic signature for both classification as well as determining track, speed and depth. He can pass visual information such as buoy pointers or, if using active buoys, range rings and doppler rates. Changes in speed, track or depth are passed verbally to the crew. In lieu of ASW operations, the SENSO can reduce crew workload by taking over one or more sensors or operating the Naval Tactical Data Systems (NTDS) Link-11*

ABOVE

With a flurry of steam under its belly, a Viking prepares to meet the end of the deck. Every carrier launch is thrilling, but surprisingly safe since operations from carriers are governed by safety rules and constant practice. Note how the retractable portions of the flaps are painted insignia red, a safety requirement on movable surfaces

RIGHT

Free of the carrier deck, the Viking climbs away at a maximum rate of climb of 4200 fpm. The S-3's GE turbofans are virtually smokeless. The highly trained Viking crew has been tasked with an increasing variety of missions. In addition to the primary role as submarine hunter-killer, the aircraft's range capability has been used to carry everthing from captured terrorists to critical ship components several thousand miles from the carrier

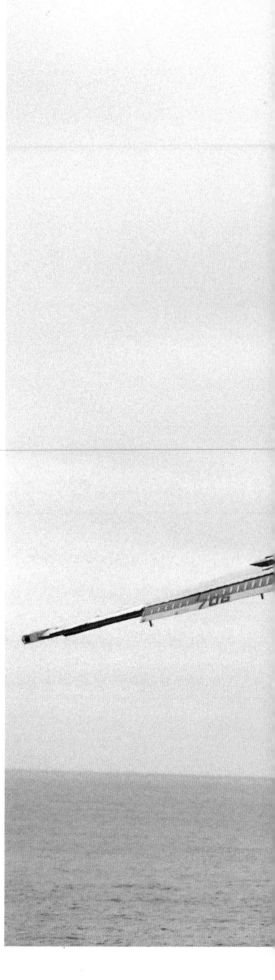

ABOVE

In the air and cleaned up, the Viking assumes a much more purposeful look than when on the ground. The 'nugget' (Navy slang for new pilot) faces a new challenge when he shows up at the Fleet Replenishment Squadron. All jet pilots are trained in formation flight, low-level navigation, bombing and air combat manoeuvring. Unlike his contemporaries in the fighter and attack squadrons, the S-3 pilot has to learn ASW. By monitoring his display and the cockpit communications between the other crew members, the pilot must maintain the 'big picture'. Trained in submarine tactics and capabilities, the pilot must keep the aircraft properly positioned. The operating environment is also new for the pilot and he must become proficient at operating at 200 feet above the water in close proximity to several other aircraft for hours at a time – a task that is both mentally and physically demanding

LEFT

Two VS-21 S-3As practice a bit of buddy refuelling. Lockheed built a KS-3A dedicated refueller prototype, utilizing the fifth YS-3A airframe. Used for a number of years by VS-41 'Shamrocks', further tanker orders were not forthcoming. However, Vikings have been modified to carry a buddy refuelling system sporting a refuelling pod that contains the hose drum and basket. The pod is carried in place of the usual external fuel tank under the left wing. Note the retractable refuelling probe above the canopy

OVERLEAF

In 1981, Lockheed was issued a $14,500,000 Weapons System Improvement Program contract (WISP) to upgrade two S-3A Viking airframes to carry the deadly Harpoon missile, expand radar processing capabilities, increase electronic support measure coverage and improve acoustic processing. The aircraft also received a new sonobuoy receiver system and were designated S-3Bs. The first one of these modernized Vikings flew on 13 September 1984. A Navy Technical Evaluation (TECHEVAL) started in late 1985 and concluded that the modifications would considerably upgrade the Viking's capabilities. A group of 22 S-3As was selected for S-3B conversion at NAS Alameda and rework is now proceeding on the remaining Viking fleet. These two S-3As are seen low over the Channel Islands off the southern California coast

ABOVE
VS-41 'Shamrocks' at NAS North Island was the sole Viking Fleet Replenishment Squadron (FRS) until the advent of the S-3B, or Bravo, Viking. VS-27 'Seawolves' at NAS Cecil Field, Florida, has begun training crews to operate the Bravo weapon system. Upgrading of all east coast Viking squadrons to Bravo standards will be completed by Fiscal Year (FY) 1991 but west coast squadrons will not transition to the Bravo until FY 1992, with the exception of VS-21 which began transitioning to the S-3B in October 1990

RIGHT
Crews of the Viking, whether it be the Alpha or Bravo, undergo a rigorous ten-month training programme that make them ultimately familiar with system and emergency procedures. The final three months of this training programme puts all four crew members in a Weapon System Trainer (WST), where individual knowledge and skills are put into practice and all-important crew co-ordination is developed and refined

ABOVE

Down and dirty, a VS-21 S-3A approaches the Enterprise *for landing. The aircraft carries one 300 gallon external fuel tank and a buddy refuelling pod. Forward visibility from the cockpit is excellent during all phases of flight, particularly useful during night landings*

LEFT

'Redtail break right!' The pilot clears his right and banks the S-3A away from the camera aircraft, showing the location of the underwing pylons and the sonobuoy storage area to advantage. The Viking's long on-station time allows the crew to act as a secure communication relay between battle groups, or as the scene of action commander (SAC) in a search and rescue mission

Heading for the cables, this view emphasizes the Viking's rugged landing gear and massive tailhook. As the Soviet submarine fleet becomes faster and quieter, Navy search area capability becomes smaller. No single unit can search and sanitize the battle group operating area for enemy submarines. Operating with various ships, the S-3 can increase the search sector size or investigate possible contacts held on ships' towed arrays

ABOVE
Viking crewmembers take a close look at the negatives and photographs of a Soviet vessel they had intercepted a few hours earlier. Vikings working with other airborne assets such as the SH-3, SH-60, SH-2, and P-3C can greatly increase track and attack capability. These complementary capabilities make the synergetic team hard to beat

RIGHT
Since a Viking mission can last five hours or longer, demand on crew skills is high. Crew co-ordination is an important concept in the S-3 community and it is paramount towards mission success and safety. Between operational deployments, S-3 squadrons use simulators and training flights to maintain pilot proficiency and develop crew co-ordination

ABOVE

Some of the 'Fighting Redtails' of VS-21 pose for the camera. With S-3Bs being phased into the fleet, it's interesting to note other Viking variants. The US-3A was a conversion of the seventh YS-3A (BuNo 157998) into a carrier on board (COD) delivery aircraft. All ASW equipment was removed and a maximum cargo load of 5750 lbs can be carried in the area previously occupied by the bomb bay, while more cargo can be carried in two 90 cubic ft pods carried on the wing pylons. Only one aircraft was completely converted, but three other partially modified YS-3As also operate in the COD mission. The US-3A has been extremely successful but the Navy does not plan to purchase further conversions

LEFT

A deckful of Vikings. Part of the crew's intensive training includes the use of torpedoes. Several torpedo ranges exist which record real time three-dimensional plots of the aircraft, torpedo and submarine. On board the aircraft, two different tape recorders store mission information. The analogue tape recorder (ATR) records signals from the buoys as well as intercockpit and radio communications. A digital tape cartridge records all system parameters such as navigation updates, buoy and weapon drop locations as well as the configuration of the acoustic data processor and ESM equipment. During mission replay, the range data is added to the information brought back from the S-3 to complete mission analysis

OVERLEAF

Its flying day over, a VS-21 Viking goes below to the hangar deck. Another variant of the Viking is the NS-3A (BuNo 157993), which made its first flight on 7 September 1989 from Palmdale, California. This aircraft served as the aerodynamic test bed for the ES-3A, a new electronic reconnaissance conversion of the S-3A. The Navy is planning to procure 16 ES-3As

Fist of
the fleet

ONE OF the most effective and faithful of all United States Navy attack aircraft recently bowed out of frontline service with a bang and not a whimper. The LTV (Ling Temco Vought) A-7E Corsair II was at the bottom end of its phase-out from fleet service when the armed forces of Iraq invaded Kuwait in a *blitzkrieg* move that effectively seized the small country before Kuwait's limited armed forces had much of a chance to react. As part of the huge American carrier force that took part in *Operation Desert Shield/Desert Storm*, the USS *John F Kennedy* (CV-67) sailed from the US on 15 August 1990, with Carrier Air Wing Three (CVW-3) aboard. As part of CVW-3, two squadrons of A-7E Corsair IIs (VA-46 'Clansmen' and VA-72 'Blue Hawks') were sent into action aboard the carrier in what will undoubtedly become the ultimate operational deployment of the type. VA-46 and VA-72 saw considerable action during Operation Desert Storm and certainly brought the long Navy combat career of the type to a very honourable conclusion.

In early 1963, the Marine Corps (who would never operate the type) and the Navy began finalizing plans for a design competition for a new aircraft that would eventually replace the Douglas A-4 Skyhawk in the light attack mission. On 17 May 1963, the competition was initiated, but only four companies submitted proposals for what would be a very lucrative contract. After examining the proposals, the Navy selected LTV's design study for a workhorse warrior of not particularly attractive aspect.

One of the main influences that LTV had over the Navy was that its proposal would utilize the very successful LTV F-8 Crusader supersonic fighter as a working basis for the attack design. Although the new aircraft looked a bit like a very stubby rendition of the elegant Crusader, no interchangeable parts were utilized and designers had to come up with many new features that were needed for the specific attack mission. For example; the new aircraft (designated the A-7, Vought Model Number V-463) would not have an afterburner; would have outboard ailerons; would mount a wing that was fixed (the angle of incidence could be changed on the F-8) and have less sweep-back; along with a shorter fuselage. Also, given the rigours of the attack mission, the design would have a greatly strengthened structure and eight weapon stations would have to carry a load of ordnance comprising some 15,000 lbs. The design of the A-7 called for the aircraft to carry just about every possible

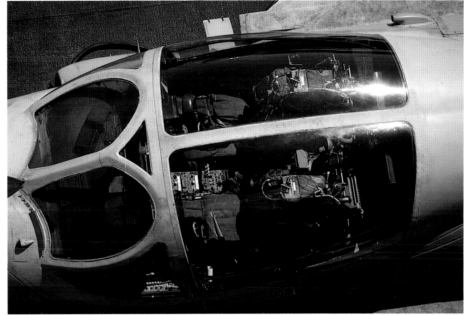

ABOVE

In this view of an Intruder cockpit, the Martin-Baker ejection seats are clearly visible along with the U-shaped handles atop the headrests. In the event of an ejection, the crewmember has the choice of either grabbing a handle located between his legs or reaching overhead for the U-shaped cord. The decision for an ejection usually happens very, very quickly but if there is time the overhead method is better because it straightens the spine while pulling a nylon visor over the face, thus reducing the chance of injury

LEFT

The massive bubble canopy on the Intruder affords the two-man crew excellent visibility. Although the basic design of the Intruder is well over 30 years old, the attack aircraft is still one of the most effective weapons in the naval inventory and, after the cancellation of the A-12 'stealth' attack aircraft in early 1991, there is no direct replacement for the Intruder which is suffering from a number of fatigue-related problems

PREVIOUS PAGES

Naval strike power at its best on the deck of the Enterprise *– Grumman A-6Es from VA-95 'Green Lizards' and a lone LTV A-7E from VA-22 'Fighting Redcocks' are prepared for flight. Enthusiasts of naval aviation will sadly note the dull paint schemes of these attack aircraft which, during the 1970s, carried some of the most colourful markings in the fleet*

An EA-6B ICAP II from VAQ-135 'Black Ravens' and a VA-95 KA-6D are prepared for launch. What is interesting about this photograph is the drastic difference in camouflage schemes, the Prowler wearing the newer TPS scheme, while the Intruder is finished in the much earlier non-specular Federal Standard (FS) 36440 grey over FS 17875 gloss white, although the KA-6D is fitted with TPS auxiliary fuel tanks. The gold tint to the canopy of the Prowler is quite noticeable. On modern combat aircraft, the canopy is usually the largest radar reflector (a close examination of the F-117A canopy will reveal all the design work that went into reducing or eliminating the unit's radar vulnerability) and the infusion of gold into the plexiglass helps reduce the Prowler's canopy radar signature

Final checks completed, a 'Green Lizard' Intruder is ready for the catapult. A KA-6D has an empty weight of 26,563 lbs, a loaded weight of 54,600 lbs and a maximum weight of 60,400 lbs – the maximum figure giving an idea of the lifting power of the Intruder, well over double its empty weight. This aircraft wears the earlier style paint scheme and is not equipped with the A-6E's distinctive TRAM turret that houses the FLIR equipment

mix of ordnance the Navy had in stock and the plane could tote over 200 combinations of weapons into combat.

Since the A-7 was to be a subsonic aircraft, the immense afterburning power of the F-8's J57 was not needed and the engine selected was the turbofan Pratt & Whitney TF30-P-6 which, in this variant, was capable of producing 11,350 lbs st. Once the final paperwork proposals were approved by the Navy review board, a contract for seven YA-7As, that would be utilized for flight testing, and 35 production A-7As was issued on 19 March 1964, with production to take place at LTV's Dallas, Texas, plant.

The first example of the new attack aircraft flew on 27 September 1965, and received the name Corsair II, honouring the company's very famous 'bent wing bird' fighter of World War 2 and Korean War fame, but a name that one rarely hears a pilot use when referring to the aircraft. As flight testing got underway, more contracts were issued and a second contract called for 140 aircraft in September 1965, while a third order resulted in 17 more A-7As.

During 1966, all seven test models were flying and the type was being closely watched because the war in South-east Asia was starting to escalate. Training squadrons VA-174 'Hellrazors' (east coast) and VA-122 'Flying Eagles' (west coast) were established during late 1966 and indoctrination training for pilots began to build-up. The first operational squadron to receive the type was VA-147 'Argonauts' (commissioned on 1 February 1967) and the squadron took its aircraft aboard the USS *Ranger* (CV-61) for the first time in June 1967, a remarkably short period of time from initial design to deployment. VA-147 went into action with the A-7A over South-east Asia on 4 December 1967, the start of a long combat career with the Navy. Since the aircraft was a fairly simple design, not many problems were encountered with the airframe, but the engine did have a slow throttle response time and pilots felt that more thrust was needed.

In order to incorporate some of the improvements learnt in combat, the Navy issued an order for 196 A-7Bs which could be fitted with TF30-P-8 turbofans that had an improved static thrust rating of 12,200 lbs. The first example of the A-7B (there was no prototype as such) flew on 6 February 1968, and production deliveries to the Navy were quickly concluded with the final A-7B being handed over on 7 May 1969. By this point, the war in South-east Asia had erupted into full fury and the A-7s were urgently required for ground attack missions. VA-146 'Blue Diamonds' and VA-215 'Barn Owls' took the A-7B into combat over Vietnam for the first time on 7 May 1969, and the A-7 became a very familiar sight to Americans watching the nightly news on television.

The United States Air Force had noticed the success of the A-7 and decided that an upgraded variant of the aircraft would fill a crucial gap in the USAF inventory. The USAF wanted a number of changes, the most major of which being the substitution of the Pratt & Whitney turbofan with a Rolls-Royce Spey, which would be built under license by Allison as the TF41-A-1, with 14,250 lbs st. New and improved avionics and subsystems, including a head-up display (HUD), and 20 mm M61A1 'Gatling' cannon replacing two single-barrel 20 mm weapons featured on the A and B models, also constituted some of the changes. Additional systems protection, new hydraulics and anti-skid brakes also helped make the A-7D a most effective warplane (the USAF purchased 459 aircraft). The Navy took note of these modifications and also decided that the A-7D would be an excellent addition to the fleet, ordering a total of 535 examples, known as the A-7E.

However, production difficulties with the Allison powerplant saw the first 67 A-7Es delivered with the TF-30-P-8 engine and the designation on these aircraft was changed to A-7C. The first 'real' A-7E with the Navy's TF41-A-2 turbofan flew on 25 November 1968, and the type went into action aboard the USS *America* (CV-66) with VA-146 and VA-147 during May 1970.

Both the Navy and the Air Force felt a need existed for dual-control variant of the A-7 and an A-7E airframe was modified and lengthened to include a second seat and full instrument panel. At first this aircraft was designated YA-7H, but this was changed to YA-7E, and further modified to TA-7C after the Navy decided to have 60 stored A-7B and A-7C aircraft converted (the USAF opting for 30 new-build A-7K dual-control aircraft). The modification programme began in mid-1975, and the airframes were given a thorough over-haul during the conversion process, but the Navy decided to retain the original TF30 engines. In 1985, the Navy put 49 TA-7Cs back into overhaul and during this time the more powerful TF41 engines were fitted.

At peak service during the early to mid-1980s, Corsair IIs equipped 22 Navy squadrons, but some of the units were already transitioning to the McDonnell Douglas F/A-18 Hornet. It was originally thought that the A-7E would soldier on well into the 1990s, but the decreasing defence budget, plus additional avail-ability of Hornets, meant that the A-7E would be phased out of operational service much more quickly.

While the Gulf War will probably be the final operational deployment by an A-7 squadron, the type will continue to serve on in specialized roles with the Navy. For example, some of the TA-7Cs were modified to carry up to five different ECM pods to simulate various enemy threats, these airframes being redesignated EA-7Ls and flown (usually with red stars) in conjunction with a wide variety of Navy operational training requirements. Other two-seaters will undoubtedly continue on in specialized roles. Greece and Portugal operate A-7s, and there is a possibility that surplus overhauled airframes will eventually be offered to friendly foreign nations.

The other 'fist of the fleet' aboard the *Enterprise* at the time of our visit was the Grumman A-6E/KA-6D Intruder of recent film fame in Paramount's *Flight of the Intruder*, based on a novel by Stephen Coontz. One of the hardest-hitting of all strike aircraft, the Intruder is also one of the longest running production combat aircraft, still being built over thirty years after the prototype first flew.

The creation of the Intruder came about from a Navy request for an aircraft which would replace the magnificent Douglas A-1 Skyraider, otherwise known as the 'Flying Dump Truck'. The new aircraft would have to have all-weather capabilities, carry a crew of two, be able to perform short take-offs and land-ings, and have a top speed of at least 500 knots along with a combat mission radius of 300 nautical miles. Oddly, the Navy left the choice of engine (jet or turboprop), and the number of powerplants needed, to the manufacturers. This certainly allowed a goodly amount of design creativity, but the Navy *did* specify that the winning bidder be responsible for the entire weapon system package and not just the airframe – this being a first-time occurence.

What the Navy wanted was formidable, but eight airframe builders were interested enough to supply the service with their concepts of what form the new strike aircraft should take. When proposals were submitted to the Navy during August 1947, a Grumman team led by Larry Mead had undertaken a number of studies before finalizing on Grumman Design 128Q. Some of these paper plans included a twin-engined turbo-prop and a twin turbojet with the wing built in an 'M' configuration. However, Design 128Q settled on a purpose-ful, if not very attractive, aircraft that had two Pratt & Whitney J52 turbojets mounted in the lower fuselage with long tail pipes that could be swivelled down-

ABOVE RIGHT
With flaps down, a KA-6D refueller from VA-95 is prepared for launch. KA-6Ds are quickly distinguishable by the large housing under the rear fuselage that covers the internal hose and reel refuelling package. The KA-6D can transfer over 15,000 lbs of fuel while loitering 150 nautical miles from the Enterprise

RIGHT
Head-on view of a KA-6D illustrates how the type's span can be reduced from 53 ft to 25 ft 4 in when the wings are folded. The KA-6D is fitted with four 400 gallon fuel tanks under the wings and can carry an additional tank or a D-704 refuelling pod on the centre fuselage pylon. The Intruder's large refuelling probe is fitted on the centreline of the fuselage directly before the windscreen

ward at a maximum angle of 23 degrees to aid in short field performance; a side-by-side cockpit that had the pilot sitting slightly forward and above the bombardier/navigator; and a very complex bit of equipment known as Digital Integrated Attack Navigation Equipment (DIANE).

The DIANE installation included an interconnected system comprising AN/APQ-92 search radar, AN/ASN-31 inertial navigation system, AN/APQ-112 track radar, AN/ASQ-61 ballistics computer, CP-729A air data computer, ADF automatic direction finder, IFF identification friend or foe, and TACAN tactical air navigation. After going over the entries, the Navy selected Grumman, but proceeded cautiously by awarding a contract that only provided funds for a full-scale mock-up and preliminary design.

The airframe itself would be built as strong as possible, and some of the design's curious looks came from the fact that so much equipment was packed into the forward fuselage area, resulting in the rest of the aeroplane rapidly tapering back to the tail unit. The A-6 did not incorporate many aeronautical advancements and was powered by two definitely 'old' technology turbojets – Pratt & Whitney YJ52-P-6s (in the experimental stage when fitted to the prototype airframes) capable of 8500 lbs st each. Since the aircraft was ordered before the 1962 tri-service designation consolidation, the original group of aircraft were known as A2F-1s, four of which were ordered during March 1959, followed by four more the next year.

ABOVE

Everything down and out, a 'Green Lizard' A-6E enters short finals for landing aboard the Enterprise. *Equipped with three external tanks, the Intruder is without armament. During deployments, the* Enterprise *would normally be equipped with one Intruder squadron that would consist of ten A-6Es and four KA-6Ds. On 18 April 1988, VA-95 Intruders participating in co-ordinated American attacks sank an Iranian* Saam *class frigate and damaged another while operating off the* Enterprise

LEFT

There are few experiences more exciting than a night launch from the deck of a super carrier. In this evening view a 'Fighting Redcocks' A-7E and a VAQ-135 Prowler go through last-minute checks before launch. The Prowler's electroluminescent formation light strips are clearly visible on the fuselage and wingtips. The Prowler carries two Aero 1D 300 gallon external fuel tanks and three AN/ALQ-99 jamming pods

A KA-6D and A-7E are prepared for launch. VA-22 dates back to July 1948 when the unit was commissioned as VF-63 at NAS Norfolk, Virginia, flying Grumman Bearcats. The squadron moved on to Grumman F9F-2 Panthers, Grumman F9F-6/8 Cougars, and North American FJ-4B Furys before being designated as an attack squadron with Douglas A-4 Skyhawks. In May 1990, following an around the world cruise aboard the Enterprise, *the 'Redcocks' retired their A-7Es and transitioned onto McDonnell Douglas F/A-18C Hornets with the new designation of VFA-22 (strike fighter squadron)*

LEFT

Carrying the Carrier Air Wing's (CVW) distinctive stylized NH tail codes, this 'Green Lizards' Intruder also displays VA-95's trident insignia. In the distance, a Sikorsky SH-3H Sea King from HS-6 'Indians' can be seen keeping an eye on aircraft operations. In the event of an accident, the orbiting rescue helicopter can be on the scene in a matter of minutes

The first A2F-1 undertook taxying trials at Bethpage before being trucked to Calverton, New York, for the flight testing. This aircraft was fitted with the barest equipment only and first flew on 19 April 1960, with Robert Smyth as the test pilot. The flight programme did not progress smoothly, mainly because of problems with the 'vacuum tube' technology of the equipment and various airframe deficiencies.

As the prototype aircraft achieved flight status, various aerodynamic changes were incorporated to handle problems that began occuring during flight. The first change saw flap slots added to eliminate severe buffeting during flap extension. Also, the horizontal tail control surfaces began to stiffen up when the fuselage speed brakes were extended, resulting in control difficulties for the test pilots. The fix for this problem was to eliminate the brakes from the fuselage and move them to the wingtips in an interlocked system to avoid asymmetrical control problems if only one brake extended. This system proved highly satisfactory. The size of the rudder was also increased to provide more authority during certain flight regimes, including spin recovery.

As flight testing continued, the then 'revolutionary' tilting jet exhausts were found to be of limited use in obtaining any significant reduction in short-field performance, and would actually only achieve this when the plane was extremely light (a rare condition for a carrier combat aircraft). These units were eliminated on production aircraft, but the exhausts were fixed with a slight downthrust angle.

It was not until the fourth prototype (which began flying in December 1960), that a full DIANE system was fitted and this immediately began to cause major problems, which would escalate until the type was delayed into entering service by a solid year. Improvements were hard won and the system was never completely reliable, requiring an inordinate amount of maintenance hours per flight hour. Even though the avionics were delaying the programme, flight testing continued, and the first carrier trials took place during December 1962 when the newly-redesignated (as of 18 September 1962) A-6A went aboard the USS *Enterprise* for the first time. Flight characteristics were greatly improved with the various modifications introduced on the newly-named Intruder, and carrier qualifications proceeded with few problems.

Once the Board of Inspection and Survey (BIS) gave the okay to the avionics, deliveries of A-6As to the designated RAG unit, VA-42 'Green Pawns' at NAS Oceana, Virginia, began in February 1963. The first contract for the A-6A consisted of 24 aircraft at $150.3 million, followed by a contract for an additional 43 A-6As at $159.3 million. During 1963, only a small number of American 'advisors' were in South-east Asia and this situation would soon change – along with the mission for the new Intruder.

The A-6A could carry a maximum of 18,000 lbs of external ordnance on four wing hardpoints and one centre line station. The plane could also carry 2344 gallons of internal fuel and a removable refuelling probe could be fitted ahead of the windshield to further extend its range. A-6As delivered after December 1965 were fitted with J52-P-8A or -8B engines rated at 9300 lbs st each. A number of A-6As were modified for testing various systems including a Circulation Control Wing system that drastically reduced landing speeds, but also cut down the top speed. One A-6A was modified as a KA-6D aerial tanker and this turned into a successful programme. The first KA-6D flew on 16 April 1970, and was fitted with an internal hose and reel refuelling package, along with a D-704 refuelling pod on the centreline station. Most of the combat avionics were removed, but the aircraft could be utilized as a visual bomber. With its five 300 gallon external fuel tanks (a modification undertaken in the middle 1980s now allows the KA-6D to operate with five 400 gallon tanks), the KA-6D has proven to be an extremely efficient refueller and 90 KA-6Ds were obtained by the Navy – all modified A-6As except for 12 airframes which had been brought up to A-6E configuration.

Although the Intruder has had a record-breaking production history, the type has been produced in only two basic variants – the A-6A and A-6E. However, there have been numerous modifications resulting in additional designations, including the A-6B which was developed as a 'wild weasel' suppression aircraft. The A-6B was created by modifying 19 A-models to carry AGM-78 anti-radiation missiles and associated gear, losing the DIANE system in the process. These aircraft were utilized to attack enemy radar and missile stations, and the hazardous nature of the mission is underlined by the fact that five A-6Bs were lost operationally during the Vietnam War. The remaining aircraft were eventually brought up to A-6E configuration.

The A-6C was created to fulfil another requirement stemming from the Vietnam War; the USAF/Navy Trails-Roads Interdiction Multi-Sensor programme, otherwise generally known as TRIM. The system was created in an attempt to stop, or at least slow down, the prodigious flow of supplies through the interconnecting network of trails and roads commonly known as the Ho Chi Minh Trail. Operating at night, the TRIM system allowed the Intruder crew to accurately locate vehicles with FLIR (forward-looking infrared) and LLLTV (low-light level television) and a variety of other sensors. The 12 modified A-6As also retained their DIANE system, along with a Black Crow receiver, which was so sensitive that it could pick up emissions from the exhaust of a truck. Not overly much is known about the operations of the A-6C but the aircraft were operated by VA-165 'Boomers' and one was lost in combat, the remaining A-6Cs being modified into A-6Es after the war.

The US Marine Corps had been closely watching the development of the

The 'Redcocks' operated Corsair IIs for 20 years before turning the aircraft in for Hornets. The tried and true A-7 has now disappeared from fleet use, totally replaced by the F/A-18 Hornet. During their operational career, the 'Fighting Redcocks' have been called into action during the Korean War, the Vietnam War and during the War at Sea against Iran in April 1988. The squadron saw three combat deployments to Korea and six to Vietnam. During their last combat cruise in Vietnam during 1972, VA-22 participated in the mining of Hai Phong harbour as well as intensive air strikes over North Vietnam

Intruder and realized that the airframe had great potential as an electronics warfare platform. The Marines had been using the faithful Douglas EF-10B Skynight in this role, but the old Skynight was definitely long in the tooth and extremely underpowered. The Marines wanted the new platform to retain part of its attack capability along with the main mission of EW. Twelve EA-6As were modified from A-6As, the first fully-equipped example flying during April 1963. In addition to these aircraft, 15 EA-6As were built from new. Looking basically like a standard Intruder, the EA-6A could be distinguished by a large ALQ-55 pod atop the vertical fin, along with a variety of other specialized jamming pods carried on the wing stations. VMCJ-1 took the EA-6A into action for the first time during November 1966 from Da Nang, where they were highly effective. The EA-6A, which retained the standard two-man crew and the name Intruder, would lead directly into the most highly-modified variant of the A-6.

The EA-6B Prowler, the four-seat electronics warfare platform, is basically a very different aircraft from the A-6, and not just an 'Intruder with extra seats and fuselage extension'. With a primary mission of protecting the surface vessels of the fleet, and its aircraft, the Prowler can offer immense jamming power against enemy radars and communications facilities, and aptly did so during the recent Gulf War. The Prowler can carry five powerful jamming pods under the wings, easily identified by the small 'propellers' out front, along with the huge pod atop the vertical tail. The AN/ALQ-99 tactical jamming system is the primary 'weapon' carried by the EA-6B, which is powered by Pratt & Whitney J52-P-408 engines of 11,200 lb st each (because of the more streamlined forward fuselage, the EA-6B can go supersonic in a slight dive). With the fuselage lengthened by 40 inches, the EA-6B could accommodate two additional crew members under the very large canopy. The prototype EA-6B, converted from an A-6A, flew for the first time on 25 May 1968 and the first operational

FAR LEFT
Time for a spot of bombing. A low drag Snakeye bomb is wheeled out of one of the Enterprise's *weapons holds towards a waiting Intruder. The blue paint denotes the fact that this is a practice bomb and not something you would want to drop 'for real' on an enemy target*

LEFT
The practice bombs are carefully strapped to their yellow dollies for transportation to the aircraft. The loading of real bombs is a hazardous process and great care must be taken by the deck crew to ensure that these practice drops are good for the air and ground crews alike

deployment of two Navy Prowler squadrons took place in 1972, these units supporting *Operation Linebacker* by flying 720 combat missions. The USS *Enterprise* had the honour of launching the Prowlers of VAQ-131 'Lancers' into combat for the first time during July 1972. Even at this late stage of the Vietnam War, the Prowlers made their presence felt, and the EW capabilities of this amazing aircraft were quickly realised as being a basic factor in bringing the enemy to the bargaining table. Also of note is the fact that not one EA-6B was lost in combat operations during the remainder of the Vietnam War.

There are five basic variants of the EA-6B, with each variant offering its own form of upgrade, but to detail these would be outside the scope of this volume. Both the Navy and Marines fly the Prowler (as well as the Intruder, although the Marines are 'giving' their A-6s back to the Navy in exchange for more F/A-18 Hornets), and the aircraft has taken part in every combat action undertaken by the United States since the Vietnam War.

During our visit aboard the *Enterprise*, VAQ-135 'Black Ravens' operated EA-6B ICAP II Prowlers. The ICAP II configuration began with the 99th Prowler during May 1982, and the advanced equipment carried by the plane includes the AN/AYK-14 Standard Navy Airborne Computer, AN/ALQ-99D jammer, newer software, CAINS (carrier aircraft inertial navigational system), and TACAN data link. The EA-6B ICAP II Prowlers can also carry the AGM-88A High-Speed Anti-Radiation Missile (HARM) and the cockpits are fitted with new UHF/VHF/HF radio packages. During April 1988, VAQ-135 aircraft jammed Iranian communication frequencies during the naval engagement *Operation Preying Mantis*. The EA-6B remains one of the most costly of all combat aircraft (due to the expensive nature of all those 'black boxes'), and per aircraft cost is now over $100,000,000. However, the EA-6B is also one of the most effective warplanes.

The first A-6E variant (once again converted from an A-6A airframe) made its first flight on 27 February 1970, while the first production example flew on 26 September 1971. The A-6E has a number of improvements over earlier variants including two P&W J52-P-8B turbojets rated at 9300 lbs st each; a new central computer; new weapon release system; and advanced radar. The capability difference between the A-6A and A-6E is huge – almost beyond comparison, and this variant of the Intruder has become the standard medium attack aircraft of the USN/USMC (no A-6s have been exported).

RIGHT
Even though they are for practice, each bomb is thoroughly checked before being installed on the aircraft

After the 482nd A-6A was completed during December 1970, Grumman switched the production line to the E-model but problems were encountered by delayed acceptance trials and the line had to be temporarily suspended. Once again, the A-6E has undergone many modifications and today's E-model is very different from an early 1970s example. Current modifications include a Target Recognition Attack Multi-sensor (TRAM) turret housing Forward Looking Infrared (FLIR) equipment; CAINS; modifications to allow the A-6E to carry the military's latest weapons; and a variety of other smaller improvements.

It was envisioned that the A-6's attack mission would be replaced by the A-12 stealth flying wing. However, bungling by General Dynamics and other contractors resulted in the government cancelling the A-12 programme during early 1991, with little hope of the A-12 ever coming back to life. This leaves the Navy with a rapidly ageing fleet of Intruders, many of which have had structural problems. In an attempt to get around wing cracking, the government awarded Boeing a contract for the construction of 120 wings to be built out of carbon fibre and epoxy resin, but problems with these wings delayed delivery and Grumman was funded to build more metal replacement wings. Many of the earlier Intruders have been restricted to low-G manoeuvring, while 51 aircraft were retired pending the availability of the new units. To compound this major problem, fuselage cracks have recently been found on some Intruders that have experienced more than 2500 carrier traps, so clearly America's naval strike power is threatened and some major decisions have to be made.

With all the American military's reliance on high-tech weaponry (which proved amazingly effective during the Gulf War), it still takes man (and muscle) power for bomb loading

Grumman has proposed a more mission-capable aircraft called the Intruder II, and five A-6F full-scale development aircraft were built during 1986/87. These aircraft had strengthened airframes, General Electric F404-GE-400D turbofans of 10,800 lbs st each, and numerous avionics updates. However, funding ran out and government enthusiasm for the project was extremely low. Two flown A-6Fs and the fourth and fifth unflown airframes were placed in storage, but the third Intruder II was kept flying to test modifications for a less-costly A-6G programme, but the continued production future of the type does not look bright in the wake of recent defence budget cuts.

At the time of our visit, VA-95 'Green Lizards' was operating A-6Es from the *Enterprise*, this squadron having a rather colourful history. Commissioned on 15 October 1943 as VT-20 torpedo bomber squadron, the unit was initially nicknamed the 'Sky Knights'. The unit flew Grumman Avengers aboard the USS *Enterprise* (CV-6), *Lexington* (CV-16), and *Kwajalien* while participating in the battles for Okinawa, Formosa, Leyte, and the second battle of the Philippine Sea. By the end of World War 2, VT-20 was credited with sinking 154,000 tons of Japanese shipping.

After the war, the designation VT-20 was retired, being replaced by VA-10A, which lasted only two years before redesignation as VA-95 on 12 August 1948. During the first part of the Korean War, VA-95 was idle, but on 26 April 1952 the squadron deployed on board the USS *Philippine Sea* (CV-57). VA-95 became the first squadron to utilize the new Mighty Mouse air-to-ground rocket during the Korean War. It was also during this time period that the squadron received its new name of 'Green Lizards'.

After the Korean War, VA-95 transitioned to the Douglas A-1 Skyraider and deployed on board the USS *Ranger* (CV-61) and USS *Ticonderoga* (CV-14). In late 1965, VA-95 transitioned to the Douglas A-4 Skyhawk and deployed on board the USS *John F Kennedy* to the South China Sea. In 1966, the squadron went on board the USS *Intrepid* (CV-10), and while deployed flew 2171 Vietnam War combat missions without the loss of a single aircraft or life.

During March 1970 the squadron was decommissioned, but two years later, on 31 March 1972, VA-95 was recommissioned and equipped with Grumman Intruders. In 1975, VA-95 participated in *Operation Eagle Lift*, the squadron's role being to provide escort for helicopters being used during the evacuation of Saigon. Later in the year VA-95 attacked targets in Cambodia in support of the recovery of the SS *Mayaguez*.

After the Vietnam War, VA-95 deployed on a WestPac on board the USS *Coral Sea* (CV-43), but the next two deployments were to the Mediterranean on board the USS *America* (CV-66). On the squadron's last Med cruise, they were equipped with A-6Es fitted with the TRAM system.

In 1982, VA-95 changed carriers once again. As a member of Carrier Air Wing 11, on board the *Enterprise*, the 'Green Lizards' really excelled. During April 1986, VA-95 provided combat support during the Libyan confrontation. In April 1988, the 'Green Lizards' were the first US aircraft to drop live ordnance on Iranian shipping during *Operation Preying Mantis*.

During 1989/90, VA-95 enjoyed another successful deployment on board the *Enterprise*. In October 1989, CVW-11 participated in the largest Naval war exercise since World War 2, known as PACEX, which involved over 50 US ships, of which three were carriers, and numerous other Allied combatants (since, of course, eclipsed by *Operation Desert Storm*). The 1990 around-the-world cruise marked the end of the CVW-11/*Enterprise* combination, since VA-95, and the rest of the air wing's squadrons, were assigned to the new USS *Abraham Lincoln* (CVN-72) when the *Enterprise* went in for its refit.

ABOVE

The A-7Es operated by the 'Redcocks' could defend themselves with an internal 20 mm M61A1 cannon with 1000 rounds of ammunition located in the front fuselage, port side. Additional protection comes in the form of two Sidewinder AAMs located on each side of the fuselage. An AIM-9L is seen being mounted on a VA-22 aircraft. The 'Redcocks' were awarded the Meritorious Unit Commendation for service while attached to Commander, Carrier Air Wing 15, and ashore at NAS Lemoore, California (the unit's home base), from 1 May 1979 to 23 November 1981 for unprecedented fulfillment of the Navy-wide goals of combat readiness and personnel retention. On 15 January 1982, VA-22's operational command was changed from Air Wing 15 to Air Wing 11, which is currently deployed aboard the USS Abraham Lincoln (CVN-72). VA-22 was named the COMNAVAIRPAC nominee for the RADM Clarence Wade McClusky Award for CY-83. In addition, the LTJG Bruce Carrier Award for excellence in aviation maintenance was bestowed upon the squadron in February 1984 for their efforts during the previous calendar year

RIGHT

It's now the turn for a 'Redcock's' Corsair II to get its load of practice bombs while a relaxing pilot watches from the intake. VA-22 received the COMNAVAIRPAC Battle Efficiency 'E' for its performance in the 1979, the 1980 and the 1981 competitive cycles, making the 'Redcocks' the holder of the Battle 'E' for three consecutive years. Additionally, VA-22 earned the FY-81 CINCPACFLT Golden Anchor Retention Award for deployable squadrons of the Pacific Fleet, and the COMLATWINGPAC John L Nicholson Retention Award for both FY-80 and FY-81. The squadron won the RADM Clarence Wade McClusky Award for CY-81 as the best attack squadron in the Navy

The Corsair II is a dependable machine
and many pilots are sad to see the demise
of the aircraft from active service,
although they are pleased the
replacement is the F/A-18. This
photograph illustrates how the pilot is
positioned in the extreme forward
fuselage where visibility is excellent – an
essential ingredient for the attack
mission. The pilot is proudly wearing
the VA-94 designator on his helmet, the
second A-7E squadron aboard the
Enterprise at the time of our visit.
Named 'Mighty Shrikes', the unit
entered service as a light attack squadron
in August 1958. VA-94 aviators flew
virtually all models of the Douglas A-4
Skyhawk until transitioning onto the
Corsair II in February 1971. Named after
the tiny ferocious bird of prey, the
'Shrikes' were originally based at NAS
Alameda but, in 1962, moved to NAS
Lemoore. The 'Mighty Shrikes'
completed several consecutive combat
deployments to South-east Asia,
commencing with a cruise on board USS
Ranger (CV-61) in 1964

ABOVE

The A-7E can carry a total of 16 Snakeye bombs and achieve a top speed of 565 mph at 12,000 ft carrying this amount of ordnance. With a typical warload, the aircraft has a range of 490 miles. In 1973, VA-94 deployed on its first peacetime cruise in a decade, again with Carrier Air Wing 15 on board Coral Sea. *During this deployment, the squadron participated in support operations for the minesweeping of North Vietnam. In 1975, during the third cruise with CVW-15 on board* Coral Sea, *the 'Shrikes' provided helicopter escort support during* Operation Frequent Wind, *the evacuation of Saigon which terminated US military involvement in Vietnam. Shortly thereafter, VA-94 participated in the recovery of the SS* Mayaguez *after its seizure by Cambodia. From May 1979 to January 1980, VA-94 deployed on board the* Kitty Hawk *to the Western Pacific and Indian Oceans, including 63 days of operations in the Arabian Sea during the Iran Crisis. The squadron's final deployment on board the* Kitty Hawk *was from May to November 1981*

LEFT

With wings extended, the A-7E spans 38 ft 9 in, is 46 ft 1½ in long, and stands just over 16 ft high. In 1965, as part of Carrier Air Wing Nine, VA-94 was airlifted to Norfolk to join the Enterprise *on the carrier's first combat cruise. The squadron was assigned to Carrier Air Wing Five in 1966 and completed four combat deployments on board USS* Hancock *(CV-19) and USS* Bon Homme Richard *(CV-31). After transitioning to the A-7, the squadron was assigned to Carrier Air Wing 15 and completed its final South-east Asian combat deployment on board USS* Coral Sea *(CV-43). The squadron then participated in the first major Navy strikes into North Vietnam since the 1968 bombing halt, and the mining of Hai Phong harbour*

ABOVE

The camouflage of a VA-22 A-7E quickly blends with the grey sea and sky as the plane catapults from the Enterprise. *In clean configuration, the A-7E has a top speed of 693 mph at sea level. Empty, the A-7E weighs in at 19,490 lbs and has a maximum take-off weight of 42,000 lbs. VA-22 made aerospace history in December 1985 by successfully launching a HARM (High-Speed Antiradiation Missile) for the first such firing by a west coast squadron. This was also the first firing of an AGM-88 that was built-up in a ship's magazine. VA-22 was named the 1987 COMNAVAIRPAC Battle Efficiency 'E' recipient for its performance in the July 1986 to December 1987 competitive cycle. The squadron was also awarded a Meritorious Unit Commendation for service from 1 January 1986 to 31 December 1986, including operations in the vicinity of Libya*

LEFT

A VA-94 A-7E is carefully directed onto the catapult's centreline. In January 1982, the 'Shrikes' joined Carrier Air Wing 11 and deployed on board Enterprise. *A Navy milestone was set in April 1983 when VA-94 became the first single-engine tactical aircraft squadron to transit the Pacific Ocean from the Philippines to the US. In May 1984, VA-94 deployed again on the* Enterprise *to the Western Pacific and Indian Oceans. During this cruise, the squadron set another record by winning every operational and maintenance award that a light attack squadron was eligible to win. In 1986, on the* Enterprise *with Carrier Air Wing 11, they again cruised the Western Pacific, Indian Ocean, and the Red Sea, making history as the first nuclear carrier to transit the Suez Canal. The carrier and squadron also operated in the Mediterranean Sea in support of Libyan operations during this record breaking cruise*

ABOVE
A 'Redcocks' A-7E gets a wave-off during a landing attempt aboard the Enterprise. At its peak during the mid-1980s, the A-7E equipped 22 Navy squadrons but transitioning to F/A-18 Hornets began soon after. With reduced military budgets, phase out of the A-7 has proceeded at a faster rate than previously planned with many of the aircraft making their last flight directly to the giant tri-service storage and scrapping yard at Davis-Monthan AFB in Arizona

RIGHT
VA-94 and VA-22 participated in the sinking of the Iranian Saam-class frigate Sahand during operations near the hostile nation. American leaders termed the action as a 'measured response' to the Iranian mining of international waters in the Persian Gulf. In March 1990, the 'Mighty Shrikes' received the Battle 'E' Award for the period 1 January 1989 through 31 December 1989. Like VA-22, the 'Mighty Shrikes' traded in their faithful A-7Es for Hornets and have become VFA-94, retaining NAS Lemoore as their home base

Trackers
and haulers

FEW WOULD dispute the statement that the Grumman E-2 series of aircraft has been one of naval aviation's true success stories. Creation of the aircraft that would become the E-2 started as long ago as the mid-1950s, when the Navy began a search for a new airborne early warning/air intercept control (AEW/AIC) aircraft. Navy planners quantified a need for an aircraft that would have greater internal volume, longer range, higher altitude, and a faster speed than any other AEW aircraft then in service. The new aircraft would also have to house the Navy's Air Tactical Data System (ATDS).

Request for Proposals (RFP) was issued on 17 February 1956 by the Navy and several companies submitted designs but Grumman's Design 123 was chosen as winner of the competition on 5 March 1957. No matter who won the contract, there was a governing fact common to all designs; the aeroplane would be very large. In order to carry all the gear aloft, the Grumman design team (led by William Rathke) had to utilize folding wings that would first fold up and then pivot back towards the tail to reduce space as much as possible. Also, a large rotodome was required to house the AN/APS-96 search radar's antenna. The rotodome, mounted in the middle of the fuselage and spanning 24 feet, was created with data supplied by Lockheed who had already designed and built, but not yet flown, a large rotodome to go atop its WV-2E Warning Star. Once again, in order to accommodate space, the rotodome was designed to be lowered nearly two feet by hydraulic jacks when Design 123 would be stored in the carrier's hangar deck. The rotodome would rotate at six revolutions per minute.

The fuselage of Design 123 was completely pressurized so that the crew could work in relative comfort, and without oxygen masks, during long missions. Two Allison T56-A-7 turboprops were chosen for the design. With the installation of the rotodome, attention had to be paid to the design of the tail so that this unit would not cause interference with the radar. Since one large vertical tail would have created an obvious radar block, the design team chose a unique set of four smaller vertical tails to eliminate any problems with the radar. However, enough vertical tail surface had to be created to insure adequate single-engine control in case of a failure of one of the turboprops.

After the Navy had inspected the blueprints and a mock-up, a contract for three prototypes (to be designated W2F-1s) was issued in late 1957. The main

PREVIOUS PAGES
Up close and personal. This tight frontal view of a VAW-117 'Wallbangers' E-2C emphasizes the unusual angles that make up the Hawkeye. The huge intake behind the bulged cockpit provides air for the Hawkeye's massive cooling system, essential for all the heat generating avionics contained within the airframe. On 1 July 1974, in ceremonies held at NAS North Island, VAW-117 was formerly established with E-2B Hawkeyes, making it the newest of the Hawkeye squadrons

RIGHT
When VAW-117 was created it took Commander Monroe J Ahrenstein, a veteran of 16 years AEW experience, just 11 months to get his personnel formed into a viable squadron. This view illustrates the Hawkeye's high aspect ratio to advantage. Wing span of the E-2C is 80 ft 7 in, while the length is 57 ft 6¾ in. Height of the Hawkeye with the rotodome in the retracted position is 16 ft 5½ in

After a mission, a VAW-117 E-2C is firmly lashed to the Enterprise's *deck. VAW-117's first deployment was aboard the USS* Independence *(CV-62). Leaving Norfolk, Virginia, on 15 October 1975, the carrier cruised the Mediterranean while the aircrews familiarized themselves with the ship. The squadron had come of age in record time and not under the best conditions. Working with aircraft over ten years old, deployed on a ship based 3000 miles from home and operating without the security or support provided by the San Diego-based E-2B community, VAW-117 had something to be proud of when the* Independence *entered Portsmouth, England, on 22 November 1975. That day also marked the first anniversary of the first flight made by VAW-117 at NAS North Island*

ABOVE
The rotodome on new production E-2Cs houses the AN/APS-145 radar, a system that is vastly superior to the unit carried on the early E-2As. This 'Wallbangers' E-2C is fitted with Hamilton Standard propellers with composite blades. Note the landing lights directly under the nose radome

factor in getting the W2F-1 up and flying would not be the speed at which Grumman could construct the aircraft, but rather the ability of the contractors to design, build, and deliver all the advanced avionics that had to be crammed into its airframe.

The first aircraft, BuNo 148147, did not fly until 21 October 1960, when Grumman test pilots Thomas Attridge and Carl Albert alighted from the Bethpage runway for a successful flight. At this time, the majority of the avionics was not fitted and it was not until 19 April 1961 that a fully-equipped flight took place.

During flight testing, problems became apparent with the four vertical tails, this design feature causing too much directional control and inadequate directional stability. An 18 inch downward extension was added to the two outboard rudders but this did not completely correct the directional stability problem so both inboard rudder surfaces were locked in place. This fix improved directional stability but created an unacceptably high single-engine approach speed. The next try at finding a solution to the problem saw the designers make the left inboard rudder operational and this solved the problem. The fix was incorporated into the production line and new aircraft were built without a right rudder. Even though the design had been created to minimize radar interference, flight testing with the radar system showed that the four vertical tails were indeed creating problems. The fix for this problem was to redesign the vertical tails to utilize as much composite material as possible, thus reducing clutter on the radar screen.

Since the airframe was relatively conventional and the powerplants reliable, testing of the prototypes was straightforward. However, major problems were encountered with the avionics and these either took complex measures to fix or, in some instances, complete replacement of the unit with another company's design.

It was probably with a bit of trepidation that carrier trials commenced as the W2F was the largest of all carrier aircraft (a distinction the type still holds). As a point of interest to this volume, the first carrier trials took place in December 1962 aboard the *Enterprise* and proceeded satisfactorily.

During September 1962, the tri-service redesignation policy took effect to give a commonality to aircraft designations and the W2F-1 became the E-2A. The plane was also given the name Hawkeye, drawing upon a fictional character created by novelist James Fenmoore Cooper. Throughout its production life the outward appearance of the Hawkeye has remained basically the same, but internally many changes have been carried out as newer and more advanced avionics became available – new delivery E-2Cs are far more mission-capable than E-2As, thus giving the air wing a very effective tool.

The original production batch of E-2As (including preproduction aircraft) totalled 59 machines, with the last E-2A being delivered to the Navy on 28 February 1967. The first operational unit to receive the E-2A was VAW-11 which began receiving aircraft in January 1964 while VAW-12 began getting its Hawkeyes in 1966. These two squadrons were much larger than normal and would deploy detachments aboard carriers to fulfil AEW requirements. However, in April 1967, the Navy changed this method of deployment and created a number of smaller squadrons that would deploy aboard carriers as separate entities. These squadrons included VAW's -112, 113, 114, 115, 116, 121, 122, 123, along with replacement training squadrons RVAW-110 and 120.

The Vietnam War was increasing in intensity when detachments from VAW-11 deployed aboard carriers in the Gulf of Tonkin, the aircraft being quickly appreciated for its capabilities and quantum improvement over its predecessor,

Engines running, the flight and deck crew go through preflight checks before the E-2C moves into launch position on the Enterprise's *deck. Currently, E-2C production at Bethpage runs at six aircraft per year, although it is not known how the 1991 defence budget cuts will ultimately effect the Grumman production line*

the Grumman E-1B Tracer. However, there was a caveat to this praise. It was only when the E-2A's systems were all functioning properly that the aircraft was effective. Once on the carrier, maintenance personnel were bedevilled by a myriad of problems with the avionics and, after the first few deployments, performance of the internal equipment was graded as poor and did not overly improve during further cruises.

The main source of trouble aboard the E-2A was the AN/ASA-27 computer and a contract was issued to Grumman to come up with a fix for the problem that was deeply effecting the Hawkeye's capability. Certain electronic modifications were undertaken and the AN/ASA-27 was replaced with a Litton L-304 computer. Flight testing of a modified aircraft began in early 1969 and proved successful, the Naval Air Rework Facility in San Diego modifying 49 E-2As into E-2Bs accordingly over a period of two years. This proved to be a thoroughly cost-effective way to cure a serious problem. By 1970, E-2Bs began operations in the Gulf of Tonkin and an E-2B from VAW-116 became the only Hawkeye lost in the Vietnam War when it crashed after take-off from the *Coral Sea*, apparently the victim of an intense fire that started in the cockpit area.

During the late 1960s, the Navy began thinking about a new advanced AEW platform but ordered an improved variant of the Hawkeye as a stopgap measure until the new aircraft became available. Grumman was authorized to construct 28 E-2C aircraft and these aircraft were distinguished by the use of a more powerful Allison turboprop – the T56-A-425 of 4910 shaft horsepower each.

ABOVE

With the twin Allisons dragging their characteristic thin trail of smoke, a 'Wallbangers' E-2C executes a missed approach to the Enterprise's *flight deck. The Allisons are very throttle-responsive and give the Hawkeye, the largest carrier aircraft in the world, good performance with a top speed of 372 mph at 20,000 ft. Maximum range of the E-2C is 2500 miles, and aircraft can operate at a maximum weight of 51,933 lbs with a wing loading of 742 lbs/sq ft. During the recent Gulf War, USN E-2Cs played a vital role in co-ordinating Allied air attacks*

LEFT

Dramatic moment of touchdown as a VAW-117 E-2C recovers aboard the Enterprise, *the Hawkeye's tail hook dragging a trail of smoke and sparks as the aircraft prepares to engage the first cable. Four other countries currently operate the E-2C and these include Israel, who was the first foreign customer; Japan, whose aircraft are assigned to the 601st Hikotai at Misawa Air Base; Singapore, who operates its four aircraft from Paya Lebar Air Base; and Egypt, who uses its aircraft to keep an eye on both its Arab neighbours and Israel since all surrounding countries provide some form of threat*

An interesting off-shoot of the E-2 programme was the C-2 Greyhound. Grumman had enjoyed outstanding success with its C-1 Trader, which had been derived from the Tracker ASW platform. The first two E-2As were thus modified into C-2 COD (Carrier Onboard Delivery) aircraft and the Navy ordered 29 aircraft to be built in two batches. However, the last dozen machines were cancelled and production was terminated in 1967. As the years ensued and the requirement for COD flights increased as the number of available aircraft decreased, the C-2 was put back into production in 1982 with an order for 39 Greyhounds. The newer Greyhounds are powered with T56-A-425 engines of 4910 shp each, and the design was built to carry up to three times as much as the earlier C-1A piston-engine COD could manage (which was the last piston-powered aircraft in the Navy inventory)

This high-angle view from the bridge of the Enterprise *illustrates the bulky appearance of the C-2A. Greyhounds operate with VR-24, VRC-30, VRC-40, VRC-50, VAW-110 and VAW-120. The last two units each have three C-2As that are utilized for replacement training. The Greyhound provides exceptional service to the carriers and without the type's excellent record, critical carrier operations would be much more complex*

However, the first two YE-2Cs (rebuilt from early E-2As) were fitted with the T56-A-422 of 4860 shp each. Flight testing began in February 1972 and other modifications and improvements carried by the first E-2Cs included AN/APS-120 radar, AN/ALR-59 Passive Detection System, and AN/ASN-36 INS Inertial Navigation System.

The advanced AEW aircraft never came about and further orders for the E-2C have continued until the present day, internal modifications occuring regularly and making a current production E-2C much more mission-capable than an early production E-2C. Constant improvements have been added to the E-2C fleet, including the installation of an AN/APS-125 Advanced Radar Processing System (ARPS) with advanced electronic counter-countermeasures (ECCM) for operations in an increasingly sophisticated enemy environment. Also, a new passive detection system, the AN/ALR-73, has been retrofitted to the E-2C fleet. Currently, E-2Cs are being built with AN/APS-145 radar while earlier aircraft are being refitted. Another recent improvement has been the replacement of the hollow steel Aeroproducts propellers with Hamilton Standard units that have composite blades.

From 1989 on, E-2Cs have been delivered with T56-A-427 turboprops that offer more power and improved specific fuel consumption. With no firm replacement aircraft scheduled for the future, production of the E-2C may continue for some time to come. Also, export orders for E-2Cs may help to extend the life of the line. So far, Israel, Japan, Egypt, and Singapore have received E-2Cs.

Currently, E-2Cs serve aboard all American carriers, while earlier E-2Bs were turned over to reserve units VAW-78 and 88, these units having now received E-2Cs. During the Gulf War, the E-2C saw considerable action, providing valuable service to the Allied war machine. Since the Vietnam War, Hawkeyes have participated in other military actions including the American invasions of Grenada and Panama as well as aiding the interception of the Egypt Air Boeing 737 carrying the hijackers of the *Achille Lauro*.

In order to help cope with America's growing drug problem, E-2C crews have also been called upon to aid the US Customs Service with the interception of low-flying drug haulers. Also, two E-2Cs were transferred from the Navy to the United States Coast Guard for drug interception duties during 1987, these aircraft operating off the Atlantic coast and in the Caribbean.

Even though the design may be rather long in the tooth, the capabilities of the E-2C are immense and provide a very valuable service to the air wing since the Hawkeye can not only provide its mission role of AEW but also control strike aircraft, undertake SAR missions, vector tankers to aircraft needing fuel, provide a secure communications link, and take over air defence management duties from ground stations that might be destroyed in the time of war. Truly, the E-2C is an aircraft of our time.

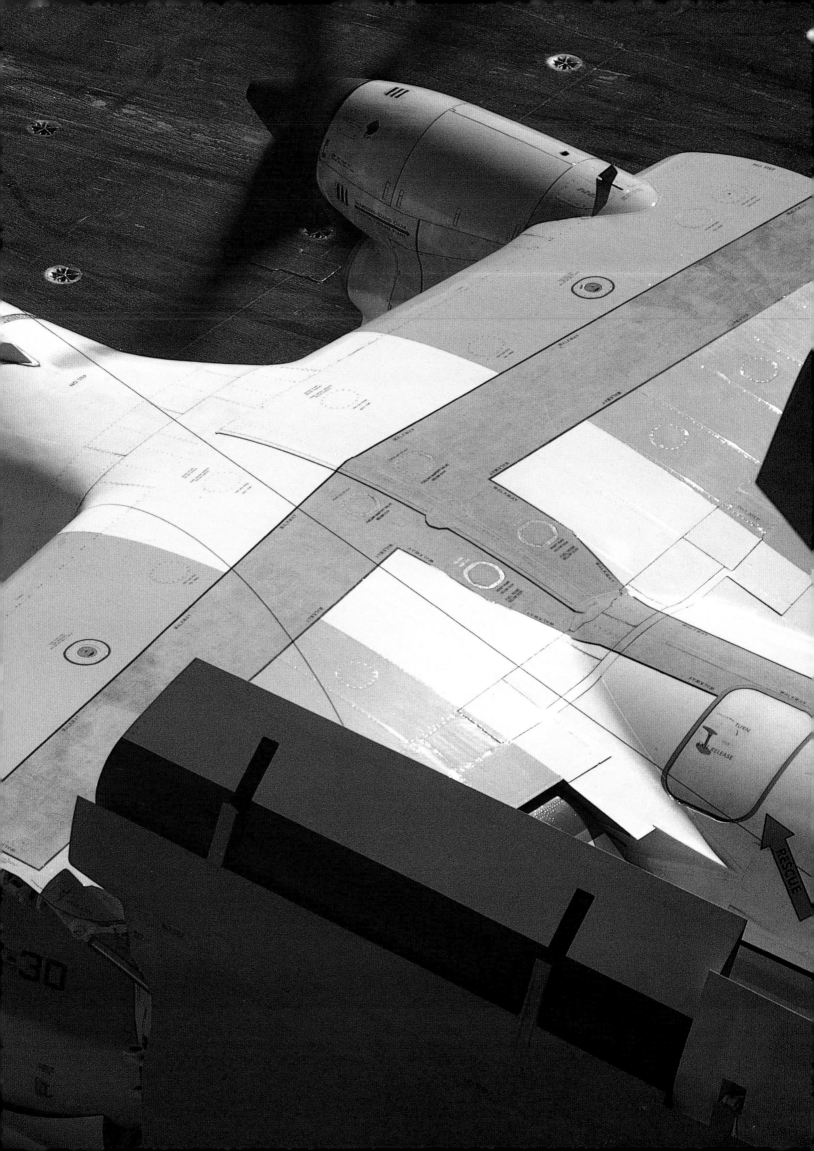

Life on the cold steel

THE DECK of an aircraft carrier is the kingdom of the young. When in full operation, the flight deck of the *Enterprise* is not unlike a scene from Dante's *Inferno*. Wreathed in steam from the ship's four catapults, figures in brightly coloured vests and bulbous helmets move with purposeful precision as a variety of combat aircraft are positioned, launched and recovered with a noise level that would be deafening without ear protectors. The physical strain and mental stress of these operations makes the deck of a carrier well-suited for the physical stamina of the young.

Although flight deck operations utilize only a small percentage of the carrier's entire personnel roster, these individuals are the most visible as they move across the cold steel in a constant state of activity. On the deck of the modern *Enterprise* there is little in the way of colour except for shades of grey camouflage on the ship and aircraft. However, a few bits of colour are interjected by the helmets and vests worn by the deck crews. Specific colours designate specific tasks. For example, a combination of yellow vest (or jersey) and helmet designates aircraft handling officers and plane directors. Catapult and arresting gear officers wear green helmets and yellow jerseys. Elevator operators wear blue jerseys and white helmets while aircraft handling crew and chockmen wear blue and blue. Green is a popular combination, being used for hook releasemen, arresting gear crew, catapult crew, maintenance crews, and, yes, photographers.

Other colour combinations include brown/brown for plane captains and red/ red for repair parties, fire fighters and ordnancemen. Helicopter crewmen wear red helmets and green jerseys while the helicopter plane captain dons a red helmet and brown jersey. Squadron plane inspectors have green helmets with white jerseys, to which are applied black and white chequerboard patterns and squadron designators. It takes a bit of practice before one can quickly identify who does what aboard a carrier deck, but once this knowledge is gained operations make a lot more sense. This form of visual identification is extremely important in combat when silent operations may be in force.

Being the first nuclear-powered carrier, the *Enterprise* made history on its shakedown cruise which started in early 1962. Although still classified, Navy officials were very impressed with the top speed of the ship, officially listed as 'over 35 knots'. At this time, *Enterprise* was home to Carrier Air Group

One (CAG-1) and this was before the designation change to Carrier Air Wing (CVW). Aircraft in CAG-1 included the stunning North American A-5 Vigilante and McDonnell Douglas F-4 Phantom II – aircraft new to the fleet and types which offered superlative performance. The shakedown cruise proceeded without incident, the ship recording its 1000th trap (arrested landing) just one month after the first!

Probably the closest point that the United States and the Soviet Union have come to all-out nuclear war was during the Cuban Crisis of 1962. Fidel Castro and his group of revolutionaries had overthrown the corrupt dictator Batista but, to the complete surprise of the American government, soon turned the new government into one of the most virulent communist regimes in the world. Rapidly establishing military ties with the Soviets, Castro began importing vast quantities of military aircraft and equipment. As part of the deal, the Soviets convinced Castro to let them install a missile system that would be capable of hitting many targets inside the United States.

This was an intolerable situation for the Kennedy administration and a blockade of the islands was announced. The *Enterprise* steamed from its home port of Norfolk and became part of the task force of the Second Fleet that cut off any shipping in and out of the island of Florida. International tensions rapidly escalated and the Strategic Air Command went on a 24-hour alert, dispersing many of its B-47s and B-52s to smaller fields to lessen the chances of first strike losses. Heated words were exchanged between the governments while high-flying Lockheed U-2s kept a close eye on the very fluid situation. As the world teetered on the brink of thermonuclear conflagration, an agreement was finally worked out that saw the missile sites disassembled and shipped back to the Soviet Union as deck cargo – an event closely monitored by American reconnaissance aircraft. The 21 November 1962 withdrawal of the missiles saw the *Enterprise* depart its station off Cuba – by which time the ship had logged over 10,000 traps, giving an idea of the intensity of air operations during this dangerous period of history.

In order to highlight the importance of the ships of America's nuclear-powered fleet, the *Enterprise* was dispatched on an around-the-world cruise in company with the cruisers USS *Long Beach* (CGN-9) and *Bainbridge* (CGN-25) – both nuclear-powered. Designated Task Force One, the ships departed on 31 July 1964 for their 30,565 mile mission. Many goodwill stops were made during the 65-day trip and thousands of people were allowed to tour the ships. However, the main point of the mission was to show that the vessels could transverse the world without being resupplied. During the operation, which was named *Sea Orbit*, the *Enterprise* maintained full flight operations, logging nearly 1600 sorties.

After *Sea Orbit*, the *Enterprise* entered dry dock for its first overhaul. When originally built, it was predicted that the cores of the nuclear powerplant would be good for only two years and an expensive overhaul would be required after this relatively short period. However, nuclear technology had progressed to the point where the new cores installed in the first overhaul would not only be less expensive but would also last 13 years – an amazing improvement. During this overhaul, many other updates and modifications were undertaken in conjunction with what had been learned during the ship's operational cruises. In accordance with improved technology, a satellite navigation system was installed, along with an Integrated Operational Intelligence System (IOIS).

By this time, the war in South-east Asia was beginning to capture the world's attention and after completion of this overhaul, the *Enterprise* headed for the China Sea on 9 October 1965. Once in position, the modern systems of the

LEFT

A catapult officer guides an aircraft to its hook-up point prior to a catapult launch. In just two seconds, the C-13 catapult (of which the Enterprise *has four) can accelerate a 78,000 lb warplane from zero to 160 mph*

BELOW LEFT

No, it's not as strange as it looks. When an aircraft is launched from the catapult, the tremendous burst of energy can blow a crewman overboard so you get out of the way quickly, and sometimes not gracefully

Enterprise, along with its vast reserves of speed, was readily appreciated and the ship was capable of setting a new carrier mission record by launching 165 missions during one day. The *Enterprise* also entered the military history books by becoming the first nuclear-powered ship to engage in combat with an enemy. The *Enterprise*'s first combat cruise was a long one, lasting nearly a year. On 5 June 1966, the carrier headed for home after having launched over 13,000 missions which saw 9000 tons of weapons expended upon the enemy. The length of the *Enterprise*'s mission was due in a good measure to the efficiency of the nuclear reactors.

When the *Enterprise* was originally conceived, it had been decided to fit the carrier with some form of defensive armament. However, this system was deleted as a part of several budget cuts instigated by the Kennedy administration. When the carrier returned from its first combat deployment, the installation of two Sea Sparrow Mk 25 launchers was undertaken, giving the ship a limited self-defence capability. At the time, it was thought the North Vietnamese Air Force might try some form of attack against the ships on Yankee Station and the defensive system would be worth the cost in case one of the attackers managed to break through the defensive shield thrown up by the other ships surrounding the carrier.

The *Enterprise*'s services were needed urgently on Yankee Station and, by the close of 1966, the ship was again engaging the enemy with its air wing which, by this time, included the new Grumman A-6A Intruder and E-2A Hawkeye. Attacks by the North Vietnamese Air Force did not materialize and the air wing was able to hit the enemy day and night. This second combat cruise did not last as long as the first, the ship returning to Alameda, California, on 6 July 1967 after logging well over 13,000 missions. Since the war showed no sign of abating, the carrier was quickly sent through an inspection and repair programme before being sent back to combat.

A fourth combat cruise was planned for early 1969, but disaster struck the ship while off Hawaii on the way to Vietnam. The deck of a carrier is a hazardous place at the best of times and this was underlined on 14 January, when a Zuni air-to-ground rocket exploded on the aft portion of the ship. White-hot chunks of metal sliced through the soft aluminium skins of other aircraft parked nearby, igniting thousands of gallons of jet fuel. Since the air wing was undergoing an Operational Readiness Inspection, many of the aircraft on the flight deck were armed and ready for sorties. The raging fire set off at least nine bombs, the explosions of which hurled aircraft and crewmen over the side of the stricken ship.

The fire crews had gone into near instantaneous action, but the fire and explosions happened so quickly that the rear of ship was engulfed in a raging inferno. The fire crews finally gained the upper hand, but not before 28 men and 15 aircraft had been lost. The repair crews aboard the carrier could, at this point, have effected temporary repairs which would have allowed the ship to continue operations but the decision was made to dock at Pearl Harbor so that permanent repairs could be undertaken. Since there was a very urgent need for the *Enterprise* and its air wing, the repairs were completed in half the time originally estimated and, on 31 March, the *Enterprise* was back in combat.

During this deployment, the *Enterprise* was diverted from action against Vietnam to a new station in the Sea of Japan. The North Korean Air Force had shot down a Lockheed EC-121 Constellation intelligence gathering aircraft on 16 April 1969, so the carrier and its supporting ships presented a show of force in case the North Koreans were considering any further actions against

The green helmet and green jersey
signify a member of the catapult crew.
Carefully monitoring the functions
of the C-13, the crewman signals that
it is okay to position a Tomcat on
the catapult

The fresnel lens system provides a backdrop for a member of the catapult crew. The pilot lines up his approach with this system, the background of which is painted black to increase contrast

LEFT

Catapult functions are monitored from this rectractable flight deck position

the Americans, or its neighbours, South Korea. After showing the flag and making sure that the North Koreans were not planning an invasion of the South, the *Enterprise* returned to Yankee Station.

When the ship retired from Yankee Station during July 1969, it was time once again to add new reactor cores and do an overhaul to inspect and repair the carrier after its intense operational deployments. This was undertaken at Newport News in Virginia, and the overhaul lasted 16 months, the carrier returning to Yankee Station in early 1971. However, the so-called peace talks in Paris began – involving the American withdrawal from Vietnam and, with the cease-fire, the *Enterprise* left Yankee Station for what was presumed to be the last time. The climactic evacuation of Saigon in 1975 meant that the *Enterprise* headed back to Vietnamese waters for the sixth, and final, cruise in that area. Covering the evacuation did not mean launching combat missions and the men of the 'Big E' had to stand by as Saigon crumbled to the invading forces. By this time, the *Enterprise*, continuing its tradition of firsts, was carrying the first operational Grumman F-14A Tomcats (VF-1 'Wolfpack' and VF-2 'Bounty Hunters'), but these new fighters did not see action.

With the pressures of the Vietnam War concluded, the *Enterprise* continued with peace-time cruises until 1979 when a three-year overhaul began. Once again, many improvements were undertaken to bring the ship up to the most modern standards. By this time, the Phalanx Close-in Weapon System (CIWS) had been perfected and three CIWSs were installed aboard the carrier. This system uses a 20 mm Vulcan cannon with a rapid-response radar system that allows close-in targets such as cruise missiles to be destroyed before hitting the ship. However, this is a 'last ditch' weapon, the use of which will probably mean that some damage will be taken by the carrier from debris from exploding missiles. During this time, improved Mk 29 launchers for the Sea Sparrows replaced the earlier Mk 25s. New radars were installed on the superstructure, altering the shape of the carrier, but when the *Enterprise* rejoined the fleet, the ship was 'state-of-the-art' in regards to electronics and weapons.

The government loves to quantify specifics and the *Enterprise* is not an exception to the rule. According to the Navy, the carrier required 915 designers to

ABOVE
The setting sun highlights a yellow start cart/tug, one of the few spots of bright colour on the Enterprise's *deck*

LEFT
Surrounded by aircraft, an arresting gear crewman uses a two-way radio for communication when the sound level permits. Note how well the aircraft are secured by a complicated arrangement of chain tie-downs

draw 16,100 drawings. The materials required for building the carrier would have required 3000 rail transport cars. The four-and-a-half acres of steel flight deck could house 69 tennis courts, five city blocks, or four football fields. The ship houses nearly 40 miles of ducts for heating and ventilation, along with 625 miles of electrical cable. There are over 3000 separate compartments aboard the ship. All this translates to one fact: the *Enterprise* is big! The overall length of the ship is 1123 ft while the flight deck is 1079 ft by 235.5 ft. Height of the ship is 250 ft, whilst the hangar deck is 732 ft by 96 ft. The ship's nuclear reactors can develop 280,000 shaft horsepower, which will drive the carrier comfortably over 35 knots. There are four propellers, each 21 ft tall, which weigh 32 tons each with a diameter of 21 ft. Four rudders, each weighing 35 tons, provide directional control. There are four aircraft elevators, each with around 4000 sq ft of space. Two anchors are installed in the bow and weigh 35 tons each. The *Enterprise* weights in at 90,000 tons with a full load and carries, with the air wing aboard, 5500 personnel.

During its 1989/1990 cruise before overhaul, the *Enterprise* launched nearly 8000 missions and logged nearly 17,800 flight hours. The ship desalinated 44,020,000 gallons of water, onloaded 15,106,789 gallons of jet fuel, changed 850 aircraft tyres, served 2,464,000 meals, while the ship's dentist performed 1519 extractions!

After the Vietnam War, the next time the *Enterprise* saw combat was during *Operation Preying Mantis* in April 1988. The carrier was assigned the duty of escorting reflagged Kuwaiti tankers carrying oil in the Persian Gulf. During this time, Iran was disrupting the passage of vessels by mining free waters and attacking oil tankers. After the USS *Samuel B Roberts* (FFG-58) was damaged by a mine, a measured response was taken against the Iranian Navy by the aircraft of CWV-11 and a number of Iranian vessels were sunk, or damaged, to teach the maverick government a lesson – which it did.

The *Enterprise*'s epic world cruise during 1989/90 covered over 42,000 miles and allowed the ship to pay goodwill visits to many ports. The *Enterprise* began an overhaul in late 1990 which will be completed in the first part of 1993. When finished, a new and improved reactor will power the carrier for at least 20 years. This will give the ship an operational life of 50 years, giving several generations of crewmen and airmen a taste of 'life on the cold steel'.

ABOVE

In the din that can go on in the hangar deck when operations are underway, a whistle can be quite useful for attracting attention while moving very expensive aircraft

RIGHT

A chunk of equipment is removed for inspection and repair. The various shops located under the flight deck can handle tasks that range from the most minor to the most major

LEFT

The Enterprise's *hangar deck is divided into two bays, these sections being separated by large blast and fireproof doors. The hangar deck is 96 feet wide and 732 feet long*

ABOVE

On 14 January 1969, a devastating series of explosions and fires wracked the Enterprise *while the carrier was steaming off Hawaii. The fire raged, setting off aircraft and nine bombs in massive explosions. It was the quick action of fire fighters such as these that saved the ship*

RIGHT

Even on a cold day, it tends to get hot inside the fire-proof suits worn by the fire fighters. Fire is the biggest threat to any carrier considering the vast quantities of aviation fuels and weapons carried by the ship

LEFT

Mounted on their distinctly painted vehicles, the fire crew keeps an eye on the action

ABOVE

Working on the cold steel is a young man's job. Tremendous physical exertion is required and the hours are very, very long

RIGHT

An essential part of flight deck operations is the FOD walk, an event in which everybody is equal and everybody performs the same tasks. FOD (foreign object damage) causes millions of dollars in losses to the military every year, so the FOD walkers keep a close look-out for nuts and bolts, or anything else that can be ingested into a jet engine

*Part of the spectacular view from the
Enterprise's superstructure, with
representatives of the air wing in an
unusual moment of repose on a portion
of the ship's 4.47 acres of flight deck*

The 'air operations' that take place in the superstructure are the heart and soul
of the carrier's mission. Each step of every mission is carefully planned, plotted
and executed

Surrounded by the red lights used during night operations, the air boss and boss emeritus plan night flight operations – perhaps the most hazardous time aboard a carrier. The air boss's official title is actually Air Department Officer, and he is responsible for all flight and hangar deck operations – a tremendous responsibility

The imposing structure above the navigation bridge is the pri-fly – the 'control tower' of the Enterprise. *Also known as the 'primary', the area is home to the air boss and his assistants*

LEFT

This view of the superstructure clearly shows the angled windows of the navigation bridge with, directly below, the rounded window enclosure that contains the television camera which records all air operations

ABOVE
These happy fellows are typical of the close companionship shared by most of the flight deck crew. Safe operations come about through the ability of each crewman to rely on the man next to him

LEFT
Even though most heavy maintenance takes place below the flight deck, work is always being performed on the aircraft prior to flight, even down to a quick cleaning of a Tomcat's large canopy

RIGHT
Most vehicles, or towed equipment on the flight deck, are called 'yellow gear' for obvious reasons

ABOVE
Captain Harry Rittenour at his seat in the pri-fly where the vital operations of the ship are literally at his fingertips

RIGHT
Night operations are some of the most exciting times aboard a carrier, and the best seat in the house is in the pri-fly, which commands a superb view of the 1079 feet of flight deck

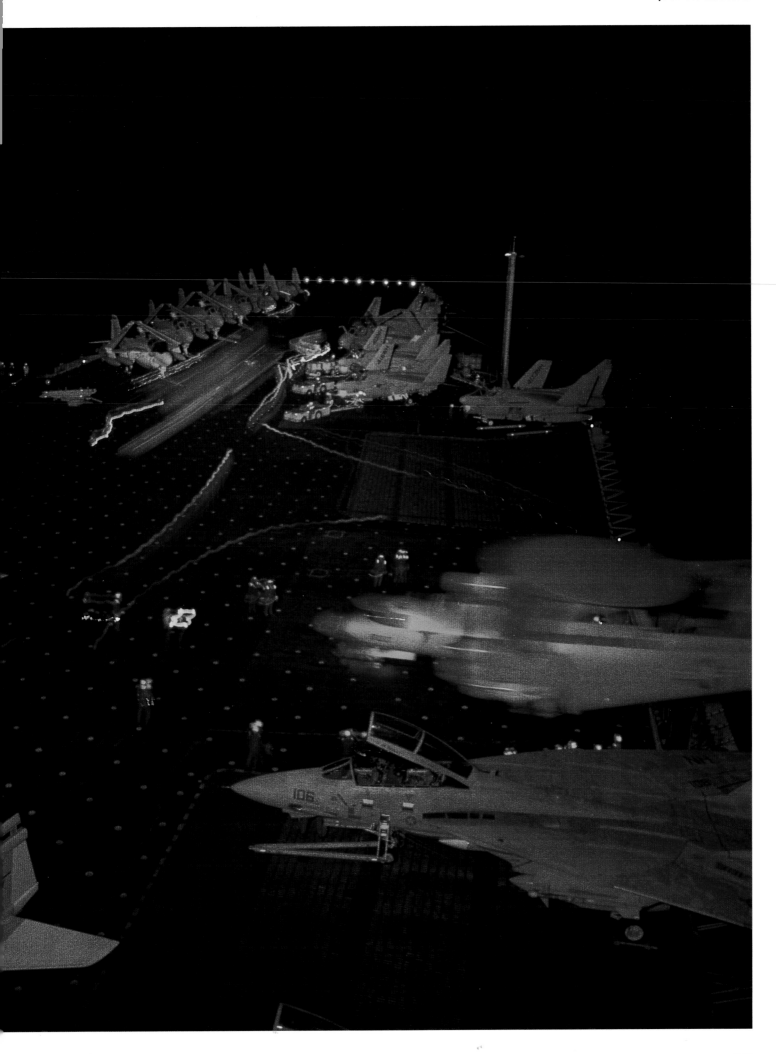

ABOVE
The LSO, and his helpers, critique each landing aboard the carrier, give advice as necessary to the pilot, and, in case of a problem or botched approach, make sure the pilot is waved off to try again

LEFT
One of the most serious jobs aboard the Enterprise *is that of LSO (Landing Signal Officer), who is in charge of aircraft recoveries and must precisely judge the quality of each approach to the carrier*

ABOVE

The LSO position is located slightly aft of the number four elevator. When flight operations are not being conducted, the LSO platform can be folded for storage. The professionalism of the LSO and his crew have drastically improved the safety record of carrier air operations

LEFT

Catapult crewmen check over the unit's cleats during a regular inspection

RIGHT

As a rising sun warms the cold steel, crewmen prepare aircraft for operations as aircraft are checked, fuelled and armed, and packages are prepared to be loaded aboard an awaiting Greyhoud COD

OVERLEAF

The 'Big E' proudly displayed on the Enterprise's superstructure has a dual meaning; the 'Big E' is, of course, a fond and historic nickname for the ship, but it also refers to the many 'E' for excellence awards won by the carrier and its crew